A Pocketful of Tickets

MARJORIE KIRKE

About the author

A fiery Welsh Dragon, who has been a grape grower in Paarl, a special constable in Leeds , corporal instructor with the Royal Observer Corps, erstwhile traveller, heritage tourism consultant and public speaker. Marjorie Kirke lives in the Calder Valley in the Yorkshire Pennines.

Introduction

It was that time of the year, mid-November 1997 to be exact – when Christmas was too far away for panic and the memory of summer holidays had evaporated. Mike and I were watching the depressing news on T.V. and not really taking it in. he was slumped in a semi-comatose position in his chair, his slipper less feet on the stool as he stared glassy-eyed at the screen and it crossed my mind what a boring couple we were becoming. Slowly somewhere inside me there bubbled an urge to escape, to go somewhere and do something exciting, stretch my wings and experience travelling. A news item caught my eye it was of a retired couple being airlifted from a ship in the North Sea. That was a bit too eventful as I am not nautical and the rolling deep would not be a comfortable experience. I also felt that I could not cope with a foreign tongue if trouble occurred. Then the weather map came on the screen. That was better I could get around Britain and the language would not be a problem. Without a lot of thought I made a decision that would upset the day to day existence of our lives for the next six months.

'I would like to go round Britain's coast by bus, would you like to come with me?' I said excitedly.

My beloved sat bolt upright and overbalanced the footstool. 'Good grief' he said with feeling 'NO!'

'Why ever not? It should be fun. We could see places neither of us have been to, meet different people, travel cheaply, backpack.'

I seemed to be losing his attention; he had reverted to looking vacant and I thought I detected a glimpse of sweat on his brow.

'Whatever do you want to do a thing like that for?' he spluttered. 'Are you quite mad? Think of the discomfort, the boredom on long bus journeys, the hunt for a decent meal, the weather.'

I was a mite surprised at his reaction. Had he not been an ex-scouter, Outward Bound Instructor, part-time soldier? Was my beloved 'over the hill?'

By this time I had the bit between my teeth and went on 'How can the weather be a problem? We'd be on buses! We could be in Scotland in May for the best weather and head south as it grows warmer.'

'And fight for seats with the rest of the tourists. There's something wrong with you girl! Just think of the midges in Mallaig. The crowds. The excess baggage we'll have to carry not to mention the washing. Don't forget the increased prices of accommodation during the holiday season.'

When I got a word in I mentioned the views; castles; museums; the historic houses and the friendliness of other backpackers etcetera

This argument didn't sway him one jot. For every pro I put forward he had a con, including the fact that I had no sense of direction and had never carried a rucksack for more than half an hour before complaining of a bad back.

He then began to itemise his idea for a perfect holiday. Skiing, mountain walks in the Alps, trips in a cable car, a 'cruise' in a hurtigruten ship. We just didn't see eye to eye on holidays, I hate heights, I much prefer to be on terra-firma, preferably speaking the same language as the people of the country I am visiting. I remained adamant now I was fixed on the idea Round Britain I would go be hook or by crook as well as by bus, if at all possible.

We were each getting heated about our opinions. I was sticking to my guns however and kept on at him, eventually we came to a compromise, he would be the organiser, the planner with atlas and timetables, he would work out the route and overnight stops for me. Best of all he would give me support if I would go on my own.

Would I take up the challenge and go the coast of Britain or as near as I could get alone?

WOULD I? YES BY JOVE I WOULD!

We set the date the 24th June 1998 to fit in with one of his business trips and over the next few days I came to terms with this decision. On the face of it, it seemed easy enough. After all, thousands of people hop on and off buses every day of their lives. I can recognise a double decker at thirty paces even without my bifocals. Also I have been buying bus tickets and leaving them in my handbag and pockets since I was twelve and I decided to travel from Hull and go widdershins just to be awkward with the sea on my right I couldn't go wrong.

Planning

At the start of the Christmas holiday period Mike contacted our Tourist Information Centre who kindly allowed him to borrow their last summer's copy of The Great British Bus Time Table which listed just about all of Britain's buses and their routes. We would have to have our own copy to refer to as the time tables went on and to check that buses still ran. Over the next few weeks Mike spent most of his free time with his nose in that book with our ancient atlas spread on his knee. We soon began to discover just how awkward it was going to be to match up connections with overnight accommodation. He kept on suggesting places where I could stay with easier and more accessible routes by train. 'Trains have toilets you know'. Was this sage advice? Occasionally when he really had a frustrating day he would wake me in the middle of the night to ask 'Do you want to stay a night in Glasgow? ' or 'Have you given a thought to London.' Preferably not to think of London at all. I hate crowds as much as Mike. I'd only been to London once before when in my teens when I was at school and I never had the urge to go again unless it was with a Blue Badge Guide. I knew without going there again that the first person I asked directions from would be a foreigner. No, I was more nervous of our capital city that fending for myself in the wilds of Scotland. He would also remind me of the times when I didn't know which way was north or when I didn't even know where we were when out walking. As the sea would be permanently on the same side I didn't see any problem at all.

I applied to join the Scottish Youth Hostel Association. and updated my English version. Their accommodation guide would give an indication of meals supplied and beds available. Scottish hostels, especially those more inaccessible were self catering. Problem number one. How much food would I be carrying?

We sent off for bus time tables and soon realised that summer services would have to fit in with opening hours of Y.H.A's and NOT the other way about.

We started to plan the route. From Hull up the East coast and round the corner. We looked at towns and hostels, buses services and coastal routes. We took turns in getting me up and around the top of Scotland as far as Durness. Problem number two. One hostel wouldn't be open until after I had left the area, I think they were shut for re-decoration.. One hotel was out of communication and the other wanted more money than I was prepared to offer. We rumbled on down the west coast of Scotland where we discovered the west coast of Scotland didn't seem to possess a bus that would take me to Kyleakin for Skye. I could if I wished, go back to Inverness and return across country Amazing! This was going to have to be a short train journey. We also got stuck in Cumbria. We chased buses hither and thither. Coastal bus services tended to arrive anything from 2 hours to 2 days after connecting transport. Times were uncertain. They obviously took travel on trust and with a cavalier attitude. We were still slogging on an hour and a half later when we discovered that there was a suitable bus – if I could get to Carlisle on a Thursday for the connection to Millom. when the once weekly volunteer driver might or might not turn up. It was that or walk fifteen miles overnight to catch the early connecting bus. Neither of us were happy with that idea. Tempers were getting frayed. Each of us insisted that Millom must have some sort of transport system. It took a whole day to discard that idea and another to come to the conclusion that I had two options. One; bus services that took me inland or travel as close as I could to the coast. As that was the whole object of the trip, coastal it was going to be – but by train.

We were still confirming previous stopovers, How long I would have in any one place Never mind sleeping and whether it would be one night or two and what about loo stops and food.

We were, by this time putting in a full day's time-tabling, collecting bus time tables as they arrived by the packet full from around the country. The one time

table that we really needed was THE GREAT BRITISH BUS TIME TABLE, which was produced on the Isle of Wight. Without this there were still great gaps in the itinerary. Panic was setting in as time was running short as the 24th June was getting ever nearer. so as to hopefully miss the midges which Scotland is famous for. Tempers were more than frayed and I could definitely hear rumblings and mutterings; even those about the jobs demanded of husbands and even at one stage divorce proceedings; I hoped that he was joking! We started blaming each other if we missed out a stretch and if we duplicated each other's moves. At one time Mike had me travelling a whole day without time for a meal or a visit to the toilet. I was on the point of rebellion and said heatedly that I would make my own way round without assistance if necessary. We had to calm down and we disappeared on solo walks leaving the other to work on the map and bus routes.

Mike was now demanding meals at the map table and spending frustrating hours re-scheduling as new time tables arrived. He took a break of a day's walking to return to find me being 'marooned' in Bodmin. There seemed to be no way out.

The people of Bodmin evidently preferred to stay where they were and not go east! However, with a supreme effort, he extricates me out of Bodmin and takes me round the south coast and into London but still with some gaps.

By this time word had got around of my trip and I was collecting advice as fast as the time tables were coming in, what to take and what to leave. Where to stay and what to visit. I did in fact purchase two packets of dehydrated meals and the dinkiest pairs of woven disposable panties. These have been around for decades and are great for holiday wear. I purchased a rucksack complete with strap for an ice pick and an eye – catching cagoule in case I might need a helicopter to air lift me home. A multi pocketed easy care Brasher drip dry pair of polyester trousers, which would carry my attacker alarm with torch. Other advice came from my aunt, who at 83 was worried about the whole thing and kept ringing me up, usually when we were up to our eye balls in paper to stress that I should not walk along beaches at night, nor to walk near cliff edges and to check all buses carefully. She must have thought that I was another Livingstone and being intrepid. Where did she think I was going? Her final words 'Don't talk to strange men.'

Mid May and with six weeks to go T. G.B.B.T.T. arrives and we heave a sigh of relief. It means however that most evenings are now spent in putting together 10 spread sheets of information. Mike decides to include the exact bus stop, as well as the route number, plus the time it would take to get to my next connection, the mileage and the bus company's telephone number. Up until the T.G.B.B.T.T. arrived and final adjustments were now made the exact number of weeks of my journey were still flexible. Now with this final and vital information I will be away for a total of five weeks. Can I really circumnavigate Britain in that length of time? Is it too short? Should I spend more time in planning for things that might go wrong? Mike has timetabled things to the minute with little room for error; if things do happen to go amiss I will be on my own. My overnight stops will be booked three or four days in advance so I could cancel if need be and take any problems as they arise. Here's hoping!

I spend the days collecting what clothing I am to pack. Not what I would like to take, but the bare essentials, including the pretty paper panties and the three dehydrated packs of food. Tea bags, sweetener and dried milk. These will go into my rucksack. A small holdall will carry mobile phone and charger, camera, notebook, my timetables and other vital pieces. Round my waist I will carry a money belt with enough money for three or four days, a debit card and phone cards which was a kind last minute thought from a friend and a bum bag on my hip.

I am ready.

Upward

DAY 1 . WEDNESDAY 24TH JUNE
HULL TO WHITBY

Mike is driving me to Hull for my start. I'm not sure who is the more nervous. I am eager to be off and yet full of trepidation. He on the other hand is wondering if I can do this without sending out messages of help. Of course it will be all right. As long as I have the sea on my right nothing can go wrong.

I have to change at Scarborough for Whitby my first night's stop. I haven't visited this interesting and historic place for some time. Apart from knowing that Captain Cook was one of its famous residents: I had also come across the event known as the 'Horngarth' or 'Penny Hedge'. It was started as a penance, now a custom, which began in 1159 when three noblemen who had been found guilty of fighting and manslaughter in church, never mind hunting without permission, were ordered to plant a hedge of stakes at the edge of the water at Whitby Harbour strong enough to withstand three tides. This custom is as far as I recall still ongoing. A diary entry for later.

My overnight stay will be in a B & B. not so much as to settle in but the hostel near the Abbey is miles away and I could not possibly rise in time for my morning bus. Not having been used to carry a rucksack on my back I am totally exhausted by the gentle climb to my B & B. Mike was right in this observation! Whether its butterflies in the stomach or hunger pangs, but I am already thinking of my stomach as I explore the harbour and discover the Vintner Restaurant, which has recently opened where I am looked after and treated to a delicious meal. Well worth including in our 'must return to' places diary. My return to the guest house is delightfully delayed by Dracula. Where else would I meet him? He is talking to school children who are enrapt by the story as much as his 'fangs'. He explains quietly to me, when no one is looking, that they are in fact a dental plate. But the children leave with the impression that Dracula stills lives.

DAY 2 . THURSDAY 25TH JUNE
WHITBY TO ST ABBS

After a hearty breakfast and good wishes the following morning I head off for my bus to Middlesborough where I have to change for Hartlepool. I can't believe that people are so chatty while waiting for buses. I am told by a total stranger about her daughter who is at university and her husband tells me about his stroke and his recovery. At Hartlepool I realise that I will not be changing in the bus station but the bus driver kindly lets me overrun my stop and lets me off nearer to my connecting bus for Newcastle These are all places that are new to me; Mike is right he would have wanted to take time to explore the town. Commuters also seem to want me to stay. The time factor and booked beds firm my resolve. We pass the Angel of The North, although seen on T.V. I had no idea that it was so large and so very brown. It is certainly impressive though. As we head out into the countryside the sun shines and all is ablaze with colour and light. We pass Morpeth Jail and Alnwick Castle and later Lindisfarne which is truly amazing in the afternoon sun. The tidal wavelets burble and rumble as they flood the famous causeway.

Berwick is reached at last and I have made a discovery. There has not been the time to have that all important stop for the loo! The day has been so fascinating with people and views that time slipped by. Now I find by checking the time table that I have half an hour to wait for the next bus out of reach of the nearest convenience, while I am perched on a wall on a lonely road and not a toilet in sight.

John is the driver of the local bus. He informs me that I can catch a bus the following morning from a stop nearer to the hostel than is indicated. Whoopee! On the journey to St. Abbs he tells me about a fishing disaster around 100 years ago. There were 30 boats and only 3 survivors at Eyemouth. He is a deep sea diver and has dived these waters many times. This area was the 1st Scottish Marine Nature Reserve where John was very active. He also does his 'touristy bit' and stops frequently so that I may take photos of fulmars and other sea birds swooping over the rocks and the crests of the waves. In fact this bit is called 'Seabird City' - listening to the raucous sounds I can well believe it. All that water is making me need the toilet even more; but how can I stop such an enthusiastic person?

My plans to take much needed exercise are shelved, as soon as I have registered and got my hostel book stamped, found the toilet and bed I have to go in search of food as my lunch was very meagre indeed. It is obvious that I have reached Scotland as the hostel is self-catering, not only that it was half day closing into the bargain.

Things have changed greatly at youth hostels since they first started, back in the twenties or thirties. Then hale and hearty walkers had up to a fifteen mile hike in between hostels. Then the hale and hearty were given a thundering wholesome meal with no choice, by the warden's wife. She would have had plenty of experience by the end of the season catering for those back-packers. Of course cars were few and far between. Anyway transport, other than push bikes would have been frowned upon if not totally disallowed.

If the warden or his wife had a farm close to the hostel a potato, a rasher of bacon, slices of bread or even an egg, fresh from the coop could be bought by self caterers.

Up until the 1980's hostellers were expected to help with the chores before leaving. It might even be a case of 'Will those on this table clean the lavatories and showers, those on this table please sweep/vacuum the lounge'. An early start was rare as everybody was busy clearing, washing up and doing other vital housework. Things were getting up dated, some would say more advanced even more sophisticated as there were nearly as many cars parked outside as people. Townies discovering the countryside had arrived in droves. There were too many visitors for the wardens to muster for kitchen duties. Families who were arriving with enough food for a siege, not content with bunking down in dormitories, were even at that time wanting 'family rooms'. Then of course they wanted en-suite shower rooms. It had even been rumoured that room service was enquired about! Evening meals were becoming adventurous if not gourmet. Forgotten were the stews, thick enough to stick your ribs together now it was burgers, pizzas and interesting salads. Also families stuck together, none of the old group bonhomie and singing or telling of encounters with farmers and their livestock. The camaraderie has slowly but inexorably dissipated over the years.

In self catering hostels there is always a dearth of food. Cars are now packed with the remnants of the stays groceries, only the most useless items are left to be used by other hostellers.

The pigeon holes on this kitchen wall for holding guests' left over food are empty. Walkers and holiday makers have not left so much as a bun. The pigeon hole that is for general use has several small salt pots all full and, glory be, a stale packet of cornflakes, one tin of stewing meat and a tin of rice pudding. This will not fill me over two meals. When nobody is looking I pilfer a slice of bread and a scrape of margarine from another pigeon hole, I can only hope that the owner won't object too much.

The weather is calm and the sea tranquil. The lighting is good as I take a gentle stroll down to the head of the cliff to take photos before going indoors to make up my bed. When I say make up my bed it's as much as I can do to throw a duvet over the sheet and hope for the best. I am not good with duvets. They are too

hot and have a tendency to suffocate me during the night.

DAY 3 . FRIDAY 26TH JUNE
ST. ABBS TO EDINBURGH

During breakfast of baked beans eaten with the remains of the stew (I hope that nobody has to starve) I have time to chat with two elderly male walkers who know the area well. They go to extreme lengths to tell me of all the places I must visit if only I had the time. One man takes his time over his cooked breakfast – lucky man - to ask me if I know that Berwick is still at war with Imperial Russia?'

'I did not know this! How can this be? Why wasn't I told? Are they about to invade?' I ask him

'Not in the foreseeable future'. he replies laconically.

'Please tell me all. How did this come about?'

'The name Berwick on Tweed was left out of the peace treaty which ended the Crimean War.'

'Did they forget to put it in?'

'Who knows.' he replied. The name was always in previous documents. And it just got forgotten.'

'Do the Berwick inhabitants worry about this?'

'Probably not, most of them don't even know about it. It's just a historical oddity.'

I leave them to it and wonder just how much more of history is forgotten and just lost as I head for the bus.

The bus stop, over a mile away, is up hill and I realise, not for the first time that going uphill whilst carrying a rucksack and bag is not to be recommended. Mike was probably right when he said that I was not much of a back-packer and would complain of a bad back. Being a regular bus service the driver knows everyone by name and catches up on the gossip. When a young lady passenger with overnight bag boards and asks the driver if he will be on the return bus on Sunday next, it sounded like a secret assignation. However he replies that he won't, but another driver will be on the route. She then asks him if he will pass her return ticket on. 'You know what I'm like', she says. 'I'll lose it before the day is out'. I struck up a conversation with Chris Connell a local water colour artist about his newest exhibition. His work was acclaimed and he was over the moon in selling twenty two out of thirty seven pictures. Although, he quite rightly pointed out, the three thousand pounds was for the work of three years.

Edinburgh Tourist Information Centre is filled to the brim with tourists of all nations. The people on duty must have an awful time explaining the same thing to different nationalities, especially if those behind the desk have a strong Scottish accent. I will have time to visit the Castle and hope to look through the Camera Obscura. No such luck, the Camera is obscured by low cloud. However there should be no cloud in the whisky distilling museum! We are ushered into a 'time machine' carriage where a young, good looking American asks me politely if he may share my 'conveyance' and reassuringly states that nothing untoward will happen. I'm not sure whether to be pleased or disappointed! We alight after our 'back in history tour' and after a wee dram of some local whisky, which my American co-traveller through time tosses off in one go and then screws his face up. I try to pretend that I am a connoisseur and sip elegantly but I too make a grimace. It wasn't to my taste either. I stroll back down the hill, purchasing a porridge spurtle on the way to send back to Mike to stir his porridge with.

The hostel is an imposing house, which has suffered the minimum of desecration, and retains its palatial hall, foyer and wall sized mirror. I am under the impression that this had been an officers' club during the Second World War. They must have had some re-unions here and some tales to tell. The foyer is crowded with late bed hunters with foreign accents. I am so pleased that I have booked a bed three or four nights in advance, as otherwise I, like those queuing behind me, would have had short shrift in the bed hunting experience. I realised too late, after I had washed a tee-shirt and socks in the kitchen sink, that there was a laundry room. I also forgot that the cafeteria would supply food so I have micro waved 2 Cornish pasties for my evening meal. The foyer is still full of cosmopolitan requests for beds, food, transport, local restaurants etc well after I have eaten, even the floor space is taken up by people squatting uncomfortably on the carpet writing postcards and phoning home.

My bed for the night is one of ten. In a average sized room we all feel that it is a little overcrowded especially when the majority of girls have oversized rucksacks. (What do they pack in there?) Someone pessimistically mentions fire regulations and we hope that these will NOT be necessary. Surprisingly, even after a trip to the loo in the middle of the night and successfully sidestepping the rucksacks, I am still asleep when my neighbour's alarm goes off at a quarter to seven.

DAY 4. SATURDAY 27TH JUNE
EDINBURGH TO ABERDEEN

I have time to post the spurtle and a wee favour for Mike's hat and then buy juice and sweets after eating a substantial continental breakfast before catching my bus for Dundee. A Fyffe Robertson look-alike complete with deer stalker and caped coat explains that he is on a day trip to Kirkcaldy and the Highland Show. He has lost count of the times he has been and thinks that this might be his last. He falls asleep on the bus before it has gone many miles. The change at Dundee for Aberdeen gives me time to enjoy a sandwich and take in the centre of the town, not to mention an urgent loo stop. Something tells me that loo stops are going to figure greatly in the scheme of things.

Great confusion a few miles on and heading for Aberdeen when a passenger rushes down to the driver to demand in an agitated fashion where exactly the bus is going? 'Aberdeen of course.' is the curt reply. As Forfar is the intended destination of the man and his wife this answer is received with some annoyance and the following request to let the man and his wife off at the next cross roads is countered with a scornful laugh, especially as the driver points out that we are on a motorway and crossings are few and far between.

Aberdeen, The Granite City, gets its name from the effect, after rain, of the whole city glistening like silver as the granite buildings, flecked with mica, sparkle in the light. However today is bright and very warm and I make a mistake and forget the instructions on how to get to the hostel. I have a map it is true, however I am a little flustered, hot and yet again requiring the toilet and a cold drink. I had totally forgotten about local bus services and walk up another hill and what seems like more than the two miles before collapsing in a heap at the door. A kind soul brought me out a glass of water as my tongue is completely furry and I can only croak. There is one consolation however: I did have the foresight and intelligence to purchase my bus ticket from the booking office for the following day as the office is closed on a Sunday. Time and days mean little when you're on and off buses and the shops remain open on Sunday. I recover my equilibrium sufficiently to join others in the kitchen to cook my evening meal. It is fortunate that, while in the centre of town, when I still had my wits about me, I managed to purchase some peppered mackerel. This seems to become my standard meal as it's easy to carry and doesn't require a lot of cooking. Plus it is hermetically sealed and will not go off on a heated bus. A Korean 'student' is struggling with a stove top, getting more and more frustrated as European cooking methods are defeating him and his rice is sticking to the bottom of his pan. He also has a tuneless way of singing. I presume that it is a national song, however the emphasis he is putting on several syllables sounds more like swear words. Two highly charged girls have their heads in the oven as they try to light it without blowing themselves up.

Sanity reigns at last and we go and eat in the dining room. Later a small collection of us remain there talking to a German captain of a trawler, or some such sea going vessel.

He had us believe that he was only thirty three years of age and had been captain of his 'trawler', or container ship, which was one hundred and fifty five metres long for some eleven years. His English falters at this point; I can only assume this length of service included his time as first officer. His major problem, he says is the number of foreign languages he has to know, to summon his crew to meals, to work harder and even to 'abandon ship'. The five of us discuss Country Rangers, the peculiarities of application forms and the Big Dipper at Blackpool. The Captain appears unconvinced as to the size or location of this even with one of the group demonstrating with a lot of hand waving. This leads somehow to modern pirates in the Asian waters. I leave my compatriots to retire for a much needed shower and to re-pack my entire rucksack, as it has fallen off the bed and the contents are in a pile on the floor

DAY 5. SUNDAY 28TH JUNE
ABERDEEN TO INVERNESS

The duvet is on the floor again this morning and realise that I have not slept well. It is a struggle to open my eyes sufficiently to wash. One of the girls, Caroline, has taken pity on me and is worried that I might get lonely. Nothing will persuade her that I am in constant communication with home. She goes so far in giving me her mother's name, address and telephone number in Loch Lomond in case I am homesick or in difficulties. How sweet is that? I wonder what her mother would have said should I turn up on her door step?

I find the local bus and head for the bus station and the 9.50 for Elgin where I change for Inverness.

The castle in Inverness, impressive as most Victorian castles are, is one of many built on the same site. It was built in 1830 to serve as both courthouse and council offices. The neo-Gothic Town House of 1882 held the First British Cabinet Meeting outside London. In 1921 David Lloyd George had to cut his holiday short to call such an emergency meeting. It says much for the man that rather then him travelling the arduous journey to London he could summon the cabinet to him!

It must be coming up for the strawberry season as there are two Polish strawberry

pickers on a strawberry picking 'holiday' I had no idea that strawberries could be found so far north and so early in the year. As their English is not too good we can only exchange good wishes and I have no option but to hope that their stay will be profitable.

First stop in Inverness – the toilet. Fortunately one of the more accommodating type. Most cubicles are so narrow that have that I have a great deal of trouble getting myself rucksack and holdall through the door and shutting it firmly. When it comes to hanging a coat or putting things on the floor it becomes a work of art.

A New Zealand couple, man and wife, who are here on holiday invite me to tag along. As they have a map from the bus station. I assumed that: a) they could read a map. b) They knew where they were going and c) They were going the same way as I. We ended up at the HO HO Hostel., which was on a par with a psychedelic hip joint, with red, green and purple rectangles covering the walls, very loud music and an odd assortment of people. The receptionist is kind and informs us that this is not the Youth Hostel, which is some way off but she would be happy for us to stay. I leave the New Zealanders there as they enquire about sleeping arrangements. They were hoping for a private room and I left them looking bewildered but hopeful. My head is still spinning from the exuberant discord and colour of the HO HO Hostel as I book in at the YHA Hostel that Mike listed in his itinerary. I then realised that I have to collect my bedding, find my room and bed and then head out looking for something to cook, as once again the hostel does not supply food in the evening. More surprising is the fact that even on a Scottish Sabbath in Inverness Sunday seemed to be a main shopping day. Marks and Spencer comes up trumps for an interesting selection of goodies that are for the sole eater and on my return I bump into two girls who are pleased to see me and hope that I may be travelling in the same direction in case they get lost. They are on a set price 'touring' train pass which enables them to visit and explore as much as they like. Good for them!

The hostel is a purpose built modern building, far and away from the vastly altered hostels that I have stayed in so far. The big drawback is that the sound proofing is not as good as it should be with every footfall above sounding as if a troupe of elephants were walking up and down. Instead of a lounge there is a 'coffee shop' area, with small tables and hard chairs. Suddenly a mobile phone rings! To a man (and woman) everybody puts their hand in their pocket. One wag calls out 'There is a shoot –out in the mobile phone saloon!' This breaks the ice and everybody starts up conversations. I take the opportunity to contact home and reassure Mike that all is well. He has been checking whether I will have time to visit anything other than John O'Groats whilst I am there. Time and tide never mind bus time tables it seems will wait for no man, or in my case woman, so any extra trips are off the cards.

It was during the night we were woken by the fire alarm. The four of us shot out of bed, collecting the things that we thought were essential for an emergency. It was later that I found that I had picked up paper tissues, my glasses and a packet of sweets. Somebody had to let me back in as I had left the door key on the dresser. At least I had my shoes on! We mustered outside and I became fascinated by the nightwear of the young male. Boxer shorts were the main garment of nightwear in all manner of designs. Several 'Hagar The Horrible' T- shirts, a few Union Jacks and, if I wasn't mistaken, a Mickey Mouse. As I was wearing an overlarge T shirt plus panties I didn't stand out in the crowd. The late comers back from the pub thought we were all having a fancy dress party. We disillusioned them quickly before they too started to strip off.

DAY 6. MONDAY 29TH JUNE
INVERNESS TO JOHN O'GROATS VIA WICK

I have the luxury of half a day in Inverness before my connection at one thirty. Unfortunately it is raining and the visibility is so poor that photography was limited.

One of my hopes was to purchase a kilt. That idea soon evaporated as a kilt would be far and above my spending power. However a visit to a kilt makers only runs to one pound and I can watch as women fold, pleat and hand stitch seven yards of material into a kilt. The time and effort is remarkable.

The weather has not improved, so as a last resort I head for the library where here in the warmth I dive into some of the history of Inverness as far back as the 14th century, when the government of Denmark placed large orders for shipbuilding. Prior to that in 1249 Matthew Prior, the Latin chronicler of that period mentions the 'wonderful' vessel which had been built for the Earl of St. Poll and Blois at Inverness.

A Mr John Pussell and a Dr. William Forbes, a past surgeon, had a dispensary for the sick poor in 1832 in Huntley Street, a facility way in advance of its time

A stone bridge was constructed in 1685 with 7 arches made from stone from the demolition at Cromwell's fort at the citadel. The cost came to £1300. This took the place of a wooden bridge that fell during an aquatic display on the river in 1664 when over one hundred people got wet but fortunately there were no fatalities. A Cromwellian officer who had crossed over the wooden bridge was heard to remark that it was 'the frailest structure that ever straddled so wide a stream'.

The Great Flood of January 25th 1849 following a bad winter took away the 1685 stone bridge connecting east and west banks of the river when the river rose,

overflowed its banks and flooded about one third of the town. The waters on the west side in particular continued to rise between two and three feet. There was pandemonium as houses filled with water and at six in the morning the bridge of 1685 finally gave way. The last person to cross was a Matthew Campbell – a little tipsy – it may be said.

Not for the first time I wished that I had the time to delve into the history of the towns I was staying in. I turned to another book. This time of old customs:

Slanderous women who had the fleur de lys branded on to their cheeks in 1559 were dragged to the market cross, made to kneel and say 'False tongue, she lied'

Punishment was dealt out for salmon poaching and the 'theft' of other types of fish by the thief having his ear nailed to a 'stake' in the market place. The ear still being attached to his head!! They didn't mess around in those days. I consider that is enough gruesome history for one day and grabbed a lunch before heading for the bus station, After changing at Wick, which is not time tabled, then onward to John O'Groats to arrive at the hostel at a quarter past five .

There can't be a journey much more depressing than that to Wick. The darkness falls quickly here and the incessant rain obliterated everything. There were just three of us going onwards to John O'Groats that evening. We huddled together in a corner of the bus stand for our connection. One of the others was an Irish ex-policeman from Surrey, also staying at the hostel from whence to commence a walk to Lands End for charity. I was very surprised that his rucksack was smaller than mine and approximately half the weight. He said calmly that he had no need of tent or camping equipment but was used to sleeping in bus shelters, deserted crofts, sheep pens and under bridges, only taking up B & B accommodation when necessary.

I am even more taken aback when he says that this is the third time he has done it, but will probably be the last as he is creeping up to his mid-seventies.

The other walker – also doing the long distance – is Robert, more relaxed about the whole thing and is taking it more leisurely and staying at B & B's on route. He has the most sensible of baggage. A cross between a golfing trolley and a shopping bag on wheels. Everything is in there including a tent.

We dive into the comparative warmth of the hostel, beating a coach full of German teens and their courier. Together they have high hopes of catching the last few minutes of an important football match. They used the German language to full effect when they are told that there isn't a T.V. in the place. The Warden likes it quiet.

There will certainly not be room in the dining hall for all of us, and Robert desperately wants a cuppa. It is then he realises that he has everything in his trolley bar tea making facilities. Perhaps the warden could oblige?

The warden states firmly that he doesn't like giving out tea bags. Robert looks pleadingly. 'Just the one.' he asks hopefully.

The warden stares at us through the grill, rather like an out-of-date post office. There is no response. Robert asks again politely. Just then two very large ladies move in either side of the warden and watch carefully as the warden takes one tea bag from under the counter and pushes it reluctantly under the grill. Robert quickly grabs it before the warden can grab it back. I am sure that I saw a malicious glint in the warden's eye when he informs us that the nearest source of food is in a pub three miles away down the unlit road. Robert is concerned that he will have to go without breakfast and I suggest falling into the arms of the landlady and looking pitiful who might give us some food to take away. However she is fully aware of the warden's attitude and after giving us a plate of chicken and chips and persuading us to try a glass of whisky to warm us up packs us up with enough sandwiches to see us through the following day.

The German group have also dined regally off spaghetti bolognaise and we each finish off a good plateful each of what was left in the saucepan.

I did not have a good night's rest. The combination of chatty people, the extra food – which I am now not used to – or was it the consumption of two drinks but my morning was not so good either.

On a better day I might have seen something of the neighbourhood. Scattered across the moorland, apart from the hotel there is said to be a visitor/centre and craft shop plus a few crofts. No doubt there would be a marker of some sort to tell the visitor that they have reached no man's land and to have their photo taken.

The Top Bit

DAY 7 . TUESDAY 30TH JUNE
JOHN O'GROATS TO TONGUE VIA THURSO

Joining my bus at 7.40 is a bit of a waking up call, especially as I am advised to be at the bus stop a good fifteen minutes early as it also serves as the school bus. Just how many children start this early?

Fortunately, as the children heading for Thurso are minimal, I can doze until

Thurso railway station is reached. A toilet and coffee – my first that day. Slightly more wide awake I present myself at the Tourist Information Office and enquire about buses to Tongue.

CONSTERNATION !! The girl behind the counter is non-plussed to say the least. She is of the opinion that such a bus does NOT run until later in the season. HELP! It probably never existed at all. I point out that the information is in the very book of time tables that she is holding. Her colleagues are getting a little flurried and time is ticking. 'Would I like to go to Bettyhill and re-commence my journey from there?' she asked. 'Not really' I replied tetchily.

As neither of us can see any alternative, my only recourse is to go to the Bettyhill bus stop. Perhaps Mike has made a mistake in collating the information, although the time table was clear. Should I ring him to check? Just as I am considering this; the receptionist from the Tourist Office runs up the hill. In a gust of apologies she tells me that my bus service (puff) has only (puff) started that day – she is very sorry (puff) but she is glad that she has caught me in time. I am more than grateful at the effort the Information Office has put in. I now have plenty of time to walk back and catch the correct bus. Waiting there already is a young Australian back-packer, Roz, whom I have met twice before and we greet each other as old friends and seasoned travellers. She is hoping to take photos of heather. I can't convince her that this is far too early, she would be better off down south.

The journey to Tongue is spectacular, with scenery stretching for miles. There is the promise of flowers in the hedgerows and blue of the sky highlights the many shades of green as we roll down in the town.

The driver points out the shops and takes us right down to the hostel at the side of the loch. I fall in love with it on sight. Another converted shooting lodge, sitting comfortably with the water lapping only a few yards away.

The kitchen isn't open but both local residents and the warden are only to happy to explain that I have come on a good day, as supplies to the shops will arrive around three o'clock, so that there would be a good choice of food. I wonder if there will be a queue or will there be a rush for the more luxurious items in the fashion of ex-pat Britain's waiting for beer supplies at Cape Town. Roz and I are happy to walk the mile back to the town and I am impressed by the two shops. That such a small town should have a Post Office is good, but to possess a bank!

That was even better as funds were running low. The Post Office doubles up as a coffee shop whilst another mini-market is well stocked. There is a garage and a church on the road down the hill to the hostel. Surprisingly perhaps there is also a hotel which serves food and is open to non-residents. It's amazing place!

I promise myself that I will come back. There are two camper vans parked near the loch. What a wonderful, peaceful way to spend a week.

Roz doesn't believe in over eating and takes herself and some cheese and an apple up the hill to gaze at the loch. I take my fresh lamb chops and an onion to the super kitchen to cook a decent meal. I have also had the foresight to buy a rasher of bacon and a tomato for breakfast. You don't get that kind of service for single people in a super - market! After supper I take a short walk to say goodnight to the loch. Just as I am going up the stairs, I am warned that Johnny, who will be driving the first bus at nine thirty five is liable to spin round at the bottom of the road and tear back up again.

What a joy it's going to be to have something hot for breakfast! This was my first 'proper breakfast' since Whitby, and I have noticed that my trousers are slightly looser than when I set off from home. I remember just in time to have my Y.H.A booklet stamped. Each hostel has its own distinctive stamp, and now my Scottish book is being filled nicely.

Going Down The West Side

DAY 8. WEDNESDAY 1ST JULY
ULLAPOOL VIA LAIRG AND ELPHIN

I stand at the side of the road waiting for Johnny who, as predicated flies down the hill and whizzes round. His little post bus takes seven passengers and he has to collect the mail bags from the Post Office before we head off into the countryside. He says that this will be his last run as he is retiring. As there is only myself in the bus Johnny can tell me a little of the work of the Scottish Post Buses. These are a vital part of the community and not only carry mail bags to the sorting office in Lairg and back to the outlining towns, but serve the farms and crofts along the way. Sometimes there can be as many shopping bags as there are mail bags. Without this service many people would not have the post nor daily groceries. Indeed as he leaves the Post Office/shop he has a bundle of letters and a carrier bag or two with addresses pinned to the handle and I am almost sure that I can hear a rattle of coins in purses. Post Buses are also used for somewhat diverse purposes he says. Very occasionally they have to recourse to carrying coffins both ways; there is a higher charge, he says, for occupancy, I have a feeling that my leg is being pulled. But it is a good story.

Johnny pulls up behind a farmer who is lifting a sheep dog into a trailer behind his Land Rover. He has spotted the dog sitting by the roadside and thinks he knows who it belongs to and will take it home with him.

'If you see a man who looks as if he has lost his dog please tell him I've got him.' It sounds a bit convoluted but I get the drift as does Johnny who obviously knows the locals.

Johnny has to stop several times to post the letters through post boxes on

people's gates and in one case a collie on hearing us, rushes down to the gate and collects the morning post and newspaper. What would this far flung and spread community do without such a service? The general good nature and caring of all the drivers and the local knowledge must be a God send to those who cannot get to the shops, bank or even chemist without their own transport. I dread to think if their own vehicle needs repair or some other emergency, like snow, preventing this Post Bus service.

Lairg is reached and I wish Johnny a happy retirement and go in search of lunch, to renew a film and just enjoy the view across the loch.

Lairg doesn't seem the right setting for the birthplace of one James Mathieson, trader and entrepreneur who co-founded Jardine-Mathieson the largest western trading conglomerate in Asia. Trading in tea and smuggling opium from India into China. Lairg is now a settled community with not a smuggler in sight.

There is a whole nest of Post Buses outside the Post Office, each serving a different area; each with its compliment of passengers and no doubt a clutch of grocery bags in the foot well. I clamber on a well filled bus with four other passengers and a small mountain of mail bags in the back. Either these tourists are foreign or they have all fallen out with each other as no own speaks for the entire journey. Normally walkers would have passed the time of day and asked me about the road ahead. I have to be content with looking at the scenery from my perch. It's all misty and grey blue. The hill on my right is starting to be covered with flowers but we are travelling too fast for me to identify. We occasionally drop off the week's groceries and offer change. The driver even has time to enquire about Mrs. So-and-so's niece and her vegetables for the next show.

I'm looking forward to Elphin. What a delightful name. I while away my time thinking what it will look like. Will there be flower strewn hillsides? Maybe small cottages at the side of the road? Or even waterfalls with odd shaped boulders tumbling over each other?

I am still dreaming when suddenly the bus stops on the wrong side of the road. The driver gets out and walks round to the back of the bus. Have we broken down?

'This is Elphin.' He says. 'You'll have to climb over the bags.'

ELPHIN!

This can't be Elphin? There's nothing here! I scramble out over Her Majesty's mail and drag my rucksack after me. There is not a goodbye from anyone.. The bus pulls away into the main stream of traffic. I am alone, in the middle of nowhere.

Where are the cottages? The waterfalls? There is nothing as far as the eye can see in any direction. There is the empty road behind us and an equally empty road to the right. Straight ahead is the road to Ullapool eighteen miles away. There is a bus shelter minus a seat and an A.A. box minus a door. This is a very minus sort of place! I will have time here to contemplate the state of the world, the economy, tourism in its various forms for the next two and a half hours before two buses will come along together going down the hill to Ullapool. IT'S GOING TO BE A LONG WAIT.

I am beginning to feel self congratulatory on my will power of not stepping into the road and waving my arms like a windmill or to lie down in the road and pretend I am a road casualty. A full fifty minutes into the wait and I hear and see a bus which is indicating the right hand turn to Ullapool. I have found my Knight of the Road!

I wave, he stops. Yes, he is going down to Ullapool and would be delighted to have company. This is the school bus returning to base. As all his passengers were fare paying he will he says accept the price of a pint instead of a fare as he has totalled up his money. My conscience is saved; I have paid my way. Norman, my driver is tickled pink when I explain my journey as we head down the road to Ullapool.

The cloud which has crept in like a soft blanket lifts in patches and the lochs, burns and crags are all around us once more. The scenery is spectacular and the shades of green, brown and ochre would fill a colour pallet. We pull off the road as Norman catches sight of one of his colleagues with his bus. Perhaps I have to change buses? His colleague, however, is taking his bus 'home' to take up residence at a Rare Breeds Farm until the beginning of the next school term. Takings are very much down this year at the Farm due to the exchange rate and both Farm and bus driver are suffering in consequence. The Rare Breeds will of course have to be fed whatever the exchange rate. Norman and I give our commiserations and we slip down and through a delightful place called Inverpolly, where he pulls behind another stationary bus in yet another lay-by to turn off major switches. 'Is this Scotland's answer to a bus depot then?' I enquire. 'Och aye', he replies casually. 'It will probably remain there several days until it's wanted again'. This is a very casual manner in which to treat a large 35 seater coach. Perhaps there will not be much traffic or indeed many highway men on the look out for such a inconspicuous get away vehicle.

We pull into the parking bay in Ullapool just as the ferry is arriving and Norman will stand by for passengers on the return journey. I beg one last favour, may I share a photo of my Knight of the Road and his steed. His colleagues, who have watched my arrival with much amusement, gladly perform this duty and take a snapshot of the two of us with Norman's bus. I'm sure he will have to take a lot of ribbing for the next few weeks.

This hostel is superbly situated right on the seafront with a narrow promenade between the row of cottages and the sea wall. Mist covered hills across the harbour. Small fishing boats bob in the water, some with red sails still hoisted.

Owing to my early arrival in Ullapool I find that not only do I have time to shop but I can enjoy the view which in itself is worth double what I shall be paying for my night's stay. The coffee 'lounge' is full of very comfortable chairs and a delightful change from some that I have encountered. The Tourist Information Office queries my time-tables but together we check my information against theirs for tomorrow. There is also a chance that I might be able to take a boat trip to the Summer Isles. 'The seals are in abundance' the lady behind the counter assures me. 'You can't miss them, don't forget your camera'. I feel that a two hour trip seal watching should not be missed and I hand over the required fare. This will definitely mean a trip to the bank tomorrow.

The view from my window was spectacular looking across the sun kissed bay, it was hard to say goodnight to it when I eventually turn in.

Our rooms seem to be interconnected, as several times a door in the far corner opens and shuts quietly. Am I imagining it?

One of my room mates has her head totally submerged under her duvet. All that can be seen is her woolly hat. The woman must feel the cold terribly. My other room mate watches the door slowly open. We are now concerned that whoever is in the other room might set upon us!! She goes to reception and HAS A WORD. When she has gone I have a mad flight of fancy and I imagine that intruders are a spearhead operation for international Youth Hostel marauders at the very least. No more is heard and we rest easy in our beds.

DAY 9. THURSDAY 2ND JULY
ULLAPOOL TO ACNASHEEN, & KYLEAKIN VIA THE SKY BRIDGE

What a morning! Although the day is slightly overcast, the sun light was giving the water such a warm gentle glow with the gentle ripples being picked out in blues and a delicate lemon yellow. What a wonderful place to have a youth hostel! Breakfast over and in a generous frame of mind I helped with the washing up.

There was time for me to visit the bank, and discover what makes Ullapool tick. I can retrace my steps and visit the Tourist Information Office; go to the library as I did in Inverness or look for the local museum which should be full of more specific interest.

The museum, once an old chapel is situated in a small lane and I am the only visitor. I can leave my rucksack at the door while I spend time immersing myself in local history. There is a video of the past industry of Ullapool where there was once a herring station, here on the north side of Loch Broom. There are pictures of women, brawny of arm, gutting fish as if their lives depended on it. Most are smiling, I suppose for the sake of the photographer, however I am sure that the happiness would have gone and determination set in once the camera had gone. The songs that they sang have disappeared into the distance unfortunately as very little was considered worthwhile keeping or recording in those days.

Thankfully the pulpit with sound box has been retained. So many churches and chapels have been desecrated by thoughtless local councils trying to up-date. There are still five long pews which are now used to great advantage in displaying visual aids. Along one of the pews, on a stand, are photo-copies of newspapers of the nineteen forties, one states in an advertisement that guarantees the cure for fits and epilepsy! They had a lot of confidence in everyday remedies then! A small area is dedicated to a school room scenario with a voice over of the class and teacher. Along with cut out replicas of children with slates and pencils and, I am sure I spotted an abacas. This takes me back to my own early school days when I too was also introduced to the counting frame. As I recall it was never a success.

The rows of beads just didn't 'add up' for me as well as numbers in a column.

I treat myself to an ice cream as I return to the visitor centre to wait for the boat. The lady behind the counter suggests that she could look after my rucksack until I return. That was a kind offer I wasn't going to refuse.

There is a coach party from Doncaster already waiting in line. Their driver/courier is the life and soul of the party, and has me joining in the laughter as he tells the most outrageous jokes. That group must have had a whale of a time during their holiday if he kept this up for a week or so.

The Captain slows down and creeps forward to allow us time for photographs. I did see fulmar, shag and cormorants. However each time the boat slid through the water, everybody on board moved to the side with a lot of 'oh's and ah's' and although I tried my best and saw a lot of rocks on which the seals were said to be resting I never could distinguish any seal from a rock although the water was strewn with jelly fish.

'That's a true sign that summer's coming' announced the captain.

We circle around and a salmon farm comes into view. Not only a draw for us but for the herring gulls, diving to snap a salmon or two as they leap from their baskets. I am a little disappointed that the seals don't seem to be very obvious when, just as we are entering the harbour, a seal with a fish in its mouth surfaces. The company at least was worth the trip and the fact that I have been truly coastal. The driver invites me to join their party for a slap up fish and chip lunch before we go our separate ways. Good Luck to the group they will have a great time in Scotland.

The bus driver taking us to Achnasheen is another one who is very knowledgeable about the area and points out waterfalls and, as we all oh! and ah!, promises that he usually stops at viewing points so that we can get out and take photos. At one of these pauses I ask his view on Nessie! Does he think she actually exists? He replies that he would like to think so, but the first person who actually sees 'her' will ruin the Legend and probably the whole area he says depressingly. His opinion on tourists in general is not at all polite. Then why does he do his job in one of the most spectacular places in the country?

I can cope with people, if I can get out and be among the hills, the lochs, the glens and the heather.' Fair enough.

The second stop has is by a sign for SKORRA peninsular, which apparently Tim Rice purchased a short time ago for two and a half million. Why? Because he liked it.

If only local drivers could be persuaded to slow or stop for a photogenic opportunity? Where I live there is some stunning scenery, as in many other rural

areas around Britain. How much a shopping trip would be enhanced.

I am the only passenger to be dropped off at Achnasheen at five o'clock. Achnasheen station is the most picturesque station I have so far encountered. That this is not a film set is unbelievable. There are hills all around that are hazy in the falling light. The village pond is complete with a single water lily. A heron, whether it is real or artificial stands to one side which adds to the enchantment. The early evening light is so gentle and misty I believe that this is what the Scots call the gloaming! even the station buildings take on a romantic quality. I can excuse the fact that one of the station buildings has been turned into a craft centre. The wrought iron bridge over the track looks like lace work. This is Brigadoon! Gene Kelly will drop by any minute and start singing. Dancers will trip gaily across the grass and the birds will sing their final song for the day. This is truly uplifting and it's all for me. I am so grateful. I am convinced that when I leave it too will vanish for another hundred years!

This next stage will be quite a change, as I am to take the train after so many buses.

It's a slow train, for which I am pleased, as this scenery can't be rushed. The train jogs its way round the Kyle of Lochalsh. I am visiting Skye, and staying at the Youth Hostel in Kyleakin.

The views from the train are the best ever. The light is muted and casts a warm glow over the dusty mauve and grey hills in the distance. Closer to hand the hills take on a warm green. At the shore's edge we pass hamlets and tiny railway halts as the train winds its way round the water's edge.

Here is a sloping horseshoe rocky island covered in trees. There a finger of land juts out, silhouetted in the distance. The water is streaked with yellow, pink, and green highlighted with patches of white as the breeze catches the water. We pass through Jean Town. A quiet cluster of houses painted white and which nudges the shore line. The houses overlook small boats bobbing at the water's edge, and all the time the trees are getting darker in the evening light with a backdrop of the wide blue sky. It's so quiet and peaceful. The loch has numerous mini islands dotted about, complete with the woolly hats of bushes and trees. The water laps the shore gently, caressing it. I can't hear it from the train but I am sure that the ripples would make a kissing sound. The sunlight sends a warm comforting glow over the whole of the loch. It is a magical place. Every five minutes the scene changes colour with the fading light. Now it has more pink, turning to red. Now a streak of mauve creeps in. It is stunningly romantic, the shades keep changing as time and the train goes by.

Some of the halts that we pass through have the remnants of once large hotels and well maintained station buildings. This is the country for the Lairds New Year's Do; the stalking party or the fishing weekend. I try to imagine the aristocracy having a whale of a time and giving the train driver the order to 'Stop at my station if you please.'

I look around the carriage to see if any of my fellow travellers are similarly affected by the sight. Not one lifts a head from their newspapers. There have been a few times when I would have liked to stand up and scream at people. This is one of them. Did they not appreciate what they had? Were they so accustomed to the sight of Heaven that they no longer looked? It was a crying shame.

The train is timed well to connect with the bus taking me over the Bridge to Skye. Like most places in remote parts of Scotland this is where Norwegians popped in, to forage, to conquer and to settle if not to just pass through. One such Norwegian was King Haakon IV who anchored his fleet here before he was defeated at the battle of Largs in 1263. They got everywhere these foreigners.

The hostel is situated by the waters edge is also full of foreigners. American women no less! They are loud and brash and full of laughter. I can't make out if they are on their way somewhere or just on a women's merry jaunt. The hostel – once a hotel – is superbly placed and overlooked by the ruins of 14th century Castle Maol.

'Will you be on the ferry on Friday?' asks the warden.

Quite honestly I'm not sure exactly what day this is. 'What is happening on the ferry on Friday?'

''The Wild Man' will make an appearance.' was the answer.

I request more information.

'He has had himself tattooed from head to foot as a leopard, we are told he has spent his redundancy money on being the tourist attraction of the year.'

Perhaps this is why the hostel is full of American women?

Not ever seeing just how far a 'leopard man' will go for notoriety I am disappointed not to catch sight of him. I tried my best to enquire later and even go so far as checking the local papers of his appearance, but to no avail. Perhaps he had gone into hiding or is a myth as big as the Loch Ness monster. I will never know.

Evening meal passes unnoticed as I rush to get outside with my camera. The sunset is amazing. The sky is full of red and bright orange. Green and crimson, blue and turquoise. It has become a kaleidoscope of colour. I sit for some time in awe, before heading for my room.

The Americans are having their time of their life well into the night, and my room mate has to curb their exuberance around midnight.

DAY 10. FRIDAY 3RD JULY
FERRY TO MALLAIG; FORT WILLIAM TO OBAN

I had thought that my ferry would start from the hostel, however the bus journey to the ferry is another round about one, taking in most of Skye. I have two holiday makers, from Skipton in Yorkshire. Kathy and Andy, who have been on Skye for their holiday and are making their way home. They know this island well and point out various points of interest as we zip up the road to Sconser. This seems to be an out of the way place but with B & B's and small hotels for hikers and hill-walkers. This area, says Andy, is still known for a battle between crofters and bailiffs who had tried unsuccessfully to evict them from the land in 1882. The road goes through glens and over streams, bypasses hills and lone crofts.

'See that lone house, there, the one tucked away at the foot of the hill?' says Andy.

I have a glimpse of a low white house in the distance.

'That belongs to Jimmy Saville'. He tells me.

'How on earth does he get up here?' I ask as there doesn't seem to be a road other then the one we are on.

'He will have a bit of a hike!' says Kathy. 'He is a great hill walker.'

They remind me also that he ran a lot in his youth. Amenities here will be very far between. I can't imagine anybody wishing to remain in the middle of nowhere at all. Some people just relish the solitude.

It's surprising what a lone traveller can learn in the space of half an hour before we reach the ferry for Mallaig. Kathy and Andy are going further on and we part company. With us on the ferry is a choir from the U.S.A. visiting Scotland who give us an impromptu rendering of the Skye Boat Song to the enjoyment of us all.

I will have time here to post another post card back home. I realise that I have not spoken to Mike since Tongue as the frequency doesn't reach so far. He will be reassured anyway that I have made it safely so far. I have a sandwich lunch sitting al fresco and pop into the Visitor Centre to watch a short film about Mallaig. This was once such a busy harbour being Britain's most westerly port, with a industrious fishing fleet. The video shows the hustle and bustle of times gone past, the number of people that Mallaig once supported, is now just another town with memories. I need to get the bus to Fort William before changing again for Oban and another night's stay. Going through Morar village after leaving Mallaig our path was crossed by 'The Jacobite' a luxurious steam train heading for Mallaig.

Fort William is at the head of Loch Linnhe, the south west end of The Great Glen which stretches from Fort William to Inverness. I feel that I have reached the Glen as

I start a long trek up the road into the town. It is a bustling town, with shops aplenty, with seating down its length for husbands waiting for wives. There is a small and interesting museum which I had hoped to visit. Unfortunately it is shut that day. Instead I spend a pleasant time sitting by the loch watching the bird life.

I had been contemplating taking the train however the time tables that Mike prepared seemed to be contradictory. 'Plan A' as a bus journey is preferable and is well worth the time spent while the views can be taken in slowly and in comfort.

Oban sits comfortably rounds its large rocky harbour, well protected from Atlantic swell by the island of Kerrera. Inland I can see towering above is McCaig's Tower. I just can't believe that anyone would build such huge and imposing folly. I have heard that other philanthropists and industrialists felt that they too should employ men who were desperate for work. It amazes me to think that anyone could take on such an imaginative enterprise as this. It is eye-dropping. It was said that it was planned and built in the late 19th century as a replica of the Coliseum in Rome. Like so many follies it was never completed as the notion ran away with the money.

The weather is still kind to me; I can't believe that I have had only encountered one shower in Inverness and the downpour at John O'Groats. The herring gulls are making the most of the fine weather by dive bombing five swans which are gently swimming near to the harbour wall.

There are numerous hotels strung out, facing the sea. Probably in this economic climate some will no doubt be turned into flats or summer accommodation. The hostel I am heading for is classed as an International Hostel; again once a very commodious hotel. International means in this case that not only are people welcomed from all over the world but is open virtually twenty four hours a day. After my evening meal I discover that the hostel possesses a public telephone. This will give Mike quite a surprise as verbal communication has been very intermittent when my battery is low or the hills get in the way. Unfortunately there is a large party of cubs staying in the hostel. I had forgotten just how much noise children can make when they really put their mind to it. I tried 'Shushing' to no avail. They continued to run screaming down the corridor. It was only when I had threatened to report them to their Akela that they screamed a decibel or two lower. At least Mike knows that I am in the land of the living.

DAYS 11 & 12. SATURDAY 4TH & SUNDAY 5TH JULY
OBAN TO LOCH LOMOND

Breakfast is surprisingly good, with a selection of cereals, fruit and yoghurt. It was over breakfast that I discussed a new branch of scouting. A young couple had some involvement with 'Super Scouts'. This branch of scouts apparently can only be found north of the border. They have a week's camping trip in the wilds each year; where they have to learn the rigours of survival including killing, plucking and cooking chickens; snaring rabbits and really involving themselves in the Baden Powell essential scout handbook. I could see that the couple really wanted to go further into telling me about the other gory details however I pleaded a tight schedule.

This hostel did some super packed sandwiches, fruit and a drink, for which I was grateful, as finding a shop and a convenience was becoming a trial as I seemed to be living on fresh air and coffee.

Whilst waiting at the bus stop an elderly gentleman asked if I would be returning for the fly past later in August. Oban, he said proudly, had been a flying boat base. A flying boat had sunk off the North Pier during the war, and on the 29th August 1998 there would be an exhibition and if I understood him the flying boat would be lifted and re-fitted. He was getting quite excited about it and I wished again that my stay could have coincided with what would be a truly momentous occasion.

My bus to Tynebroom passes Loch Awe on the north side of Loch Fyne. Loch Awe, although narrow has tiny islands with mini castles on each. Were they for holiday accommodation or did each one hold a 'court' of people each with their own clan? A total mystery! The clouds have their ski caps on and the tops of hills and crags peep coyly through the mists. We drive on through Cairndow which I am almost sure, but I might be mistaken, has a place name that says 'Rest and Be Thankful' My vision of hills and water, glens and sky is making me dizzy, there is so much to take in. Plus the road is excessively busy and traffic builds up behind us as we approach Loch Lomond Hostel.

I survive the suicidal dash across the road and I have ten minutes of easy walking up the long drive until I am confronted by the impressive sight of 'Auchendennan House'. This hostel is not just impressive, it takes my breath away! There is a sweeping circular carriage drive. A huge door way and the 'House' has turrets and windows everywhere.

The hallway is more of a reception room with panelling and sculptured ceiling with a fireplace large enough to roast an ox is in front of me. Stained glass windows let in a motley of coloured light so that the whole room is bright and cheerful.

Now Mike has stayed here before and has told me what I should expect from the hospitality. He said that the food was plentiful. I'm sure he mentioned things like haggis or venison or some such delicacy. He joined in with Scottish dancing one evening as he is light of foot. He said that the whole experience took some beating.

All I can say is that it must have been a long long time since he was there. Or else his imagination ran away with him.

Although there was a sign over the reception desk declaring the dinner hour, there was no dinner. There was no dancing either. I am here for two nights without a vestige of food and I have a momentary panic until a receptionist says that she will be finishing shortly and will happily take me across the loch to Balloch so that I can shop. I could have fallen on her shoulder and cried in relief. The two mile walk back will be worth it.

Meanwhile someone will show me to my room. We walk several miles of corridor and climb many sets of stairs until I am shown into a room way above in the attic with A VIEW. I can look over the garden towards the loch. This was probably a

maid's room and with just enough room for two sets of double bunks. Who cares that I will have to get up fifteen minutes early for breakfast if I can wake up to this every morning? Breakfast is shared with more Americans and other fellow travellers. I feel that I should be breakfasting with minor aristocracy at the very least. We are offered a meagre breakfast of the continental variety. A pity that I do not have the luxury of salmon or smoked haddock as would have been the norm many generations ago.

I am going to relish the full day here, relaxing, reading and taking in the atmosphere as well as catching up with washing. This has been piling up in my rucksack and definitely needs airing at the very least.

In the hall I find lots of information on the history of Auchendennan House. It was built in 1866 on the original site of King Robert the Bruce's hunting lodge; the architect being one John Burnett, who designed the Clydesdale Bank in Glasgow. The plaster work, as I suspected has as Italian influence especially in the Upper Hall, once the banqueting hall. The fountain at the front of the house was constructed in 1888 with an impressive bronze eagle at the centre. Sadly in 1973 this disappeared. The Scottish Youth Hostel Association purchased the house in 1946 and I must say have treated the house with respect and care by leaving walls and ceiling entirely alone. What is striking is the motto above the gallery rail. 'Peace be with all who neath this rooftree rest.'. Long may this house continue in the safe hands of the Association.

A walk round the grounds, now sadly overgrown I discover what looks like an ice house tucked away in the shrubbery. I ask about its existence but no-one seems to know of its whereabouts or even when it was last used.

My laundry done and dripping well and I make numerous phone calls for onward accommodation in Dumfries. This will be a change as my overnight stay will be in a guest house.

To my disgust I find that some bright spark, who took an opportunity when it was offered helped themselves to some of my food and I hope whoever it was choked on it! So I have no choice but to make the four mile round trip back to Balloch for replenishments.

I sat awhile on the other side of the loch as a small group of girls are putting on a display of Scottish dancing watched by many including swans who are equally fascinated.

Now is the time to phone home and discuss further sleeping arrangements. Mike's proposal is to meet me and take me round Chester when I finally arrive there in two days time. He will even go so far as to pay for a night in a B & B. this is luxury indeed. Oh, for a comfy bed. Maybe even a bath never mind a good meal not cooked by myself. We will keep in touch.

My feet are not accustomed to all this road walking. Six miles in two days! I much prefer the moorland and the grassy banks. I haven't put my feet to the ground for so long since Robert and I walked from John O'Groats hostel to the pub. I shall take advantage of a quiet sit with a good book in a large and squishy chair in the Banqueting Hall. Comfortably ensconced and feeling the benefits of rest when I become aware of several American ladies entering the room. They tip-toe in and whisper to each other.

'Take a look at the ceiling Mary'

'Isn't it just wonderful Louise'.

'Cynthia, the wood panelling, it's superb. We don't have anything like this at home.'

'Isn't it just old worldly?

'It's all so ancient.' says another.

They walk carefully round the room, exclaiming at the furniture, the fireplace, the windows. They point out everything to each other as if they were either in a cathedral or a museum.

I am waiting for one of them to come and point me out as an ancient artefact.

They tip-toe quietly out again.

Washing dried I go to cook my evening meal before someone else decides that my lamb chop, vegetables and onion gravy is right up their street.

My room has another occupant. She has taken the top bunk across from me and she has left her belongings on a pile on her bunk. I hope that she doesn't snore! So many of my room mates have snored and the range of sounds cannot be described!

My sleeping bag, with pillow case joined on to one end is rather on the large size; however as I am a restless sleeper this is no bad thing. These sleeping bags are not of the one size fits all category. They can come in wide and long, narrow and long or very narrow and short and dished out willy-nilly. My room mate has unfortunately been given a very narrow one. I am now treated to ten minutes of silent comedy as she presumably thinks that the sleeping bag is in fact a duvet cover and proceeds to cram the duvet into it. It now resembles a badly made sausage. Not content with the contortions she has put herself through, she then struggles, still on the top bunk to jamb herself in as well. It was like watching a silent movie with Laurel and Hardy. Should I offer to help? Not on your Nelly. If she had sworn or yelled for help or even fallen onto the floor I might have been tempted. As it was I was shaking with silent laughter and had to turn over with my face to the wall before I made it obvious that I was watching.

DAY 13. MONDAY 6TH JULY
DUMFRIES VIA GLASGOW AND STRANRAER

Breakfast leaves me frustrated. I have come into contact with continental breakfasts before in other hostels. Usually they have consisted of yoghurt, fruit, toast and cereal This hostel however works on the economic idea that everybody should have the same. We are provided with one roll and a small packet of butter; a sachet of apricot jam and a slice of cheese from a packet plus a thin slice of cooked ham. I am in a quandary: The jam certainly won't go with the cheese. If I make a sandwich with the ham and cheese what do I do with the jam? And so it went on. Others around me were of a similar mind. The Americans are waving their hands about stacking and re-stacking their plateful. I ended up making a ham sandwich to eat later and leaving everything else.

I dice with death again as I cross the main road for the bus to Glasgow. I have not seen so many sleeping passengers before. Where they have come from and where they are heading is anybody's guess. I hope that it is the terminus or else they will have to be woken up.

My ride takes us through the country, still with curvy hills and shadowy patches as the sun moves. The smoky blue cloud formations are forever changing into shapes, figures and pictures.

The approach into Glasgow is not inspiring: maybe we have sneaked in through the business quarter? It is definitely industrial. Several run-down warehouses and other buildings that look as if they once had a use but are now forgotten. Glasgow is a City of Culture but this approach is not a good introduction. When the view is not what one is expecting I is best to have a good novel handy.

I have a problem: The lady at the enquiry office informs me, in a tone that is not to be trifled with, that my connection to Stanraer now no longer exists. We have eye to eye contact but she is adamant, and not inclined to check this on my behalf. Even when I produce my trusty timetable she waves it away with a dismissive hand. She does suggest however that there might be away round my dilemma by me changing twice in some remote town which will get me to my next stopover in Dumfries very late. Never mind missing dinner, I might even have to wake up my landlady so that I can gain admittance. Never mind that they would very likely charge me for my bed and board if I had the temerity to cancel it. I enquire about a bus that will get me to Dumfries in one 'hop'. She does this with bad grace with the queue increasing behind me. Eventually I prise from her the information as to which bus stop I need and go to locate my bus. I can NOT believe that there isn't a mode of transport to a famous port. For goodness sake ferries leave from there. How would passengers manage getting a boat? I am fuming but there is nothing to be done but to bite the bullet. I wonder if this new route will be longer or shorter than the original that was time tabled? As this is a later departure from the one timetabled I have time for a coffee and a toilet stop. These things have to be fitted in when they can, as I can never tell when I might come across a public convenience.

I am still muttering to myself about unhelpful bus station staff and the likelihood of being totally off course, so I take little notice of the places that we pass through, although some of them have delightful names. Larkhall; Kirkmuirhill; Lesmahagow and Crawford. We have a brief stop in Moffatt, which I must say looks delightfully clean, bright and cheerful. A few shop owners must have a sense of humour as two shops – one a café is called 'The Grumblin' tum' with another shop called 'the Thingumyjig.' We have passed it before I can find out what it actually sells. I have heard tell that the narrowest hotel in Britain is here in Moffatt. It sits in the High Street and measures, if the tale is right, only 20ft (6metres) wide. It must be a tight fit at closing time

Before I know it we are in Dumfries! is a pretty place, with buildings of red sandstone. I pause by the river Nith and admire the bridge which is said to be the longest medieval arch stone bridge in Scotland.

Dumfries has more than its fair share of historical facts. Robert the Bruce murdered his rival here for the Scottish throne, and captured Dumfries Castle on the 10th February 1306. Now a feeling of hunger is upon me so I go in search of sustenance. I am in luck as I have discovered a wonderful café that does 'the roast of the day'. They are only too willing to pile extra vegetables on to my plate as I am so missing my greens. While I am having lunch I discover that I am sitting in the very house where Robert Burns once lived in 1791.The row must have had quite a reputation as it was known locally as 'The Stinking Vennel. Here he was employed as an Exciseman and lived on the middle floor above a fiddle player! History does not record whether they got on, or indeed whether Mrs Burns had recourse to bang on the floor as she was trying to get her children to sleep. I know I would have been banging on the fiddler's door with more than a broom!

I am thwarted once again! I had hoped to visit the Camera Obscura. It is closed for some obscure reason. I wander round the town and take my ease on a seat with a view. This is a reflective time for me. I am almost half way through my journey; seeing places, learning things that I never thought I would. Small towns, villages, historic hostels and much of interest from the inhabitants of the places I have passed through.

One of the inhabitants of Dumfries joins me on my bench. She is keen that I should know more about her town. Did I know for instance: that James Barrie attended Dumfries Academy, and while playing in the riverside gardens thought up Captain Hook and Peter Pan? The First Recorded School cookery Class was

started here in Dumfries in 1713? She passes on information as if she were hoping I would pass an exam at the end. There was a mention of Ferro-Concrete and Post Office Stamps. Of course I knew that was where Robert Burns lived, didn't I? I am now a bit bewildered, there is a lot of information, far too much to take in that I became mesmerised by her knowledge. I was left wondering if she was a Blue Badge Guide on a day off. As a parting snippet; she asked if I knew that John Laurie of Dad's Army fame was born here? This is a town, where if one had the time you could go away with a lot of interesting information, and no doubt bore your dinner guests half to death.

We parted company and I had a light tea; my lunch was sustaining enough, especially when I am not walking the town trails.

My guest house is delightful and I am shown my room, which has a fridge with fresh orange juice already there. There is also an extensive breakfast menu list to choose from before I retire to bed.

DAY 14. TUESDAY 7TH JULY
LANCASTER VIA CARLISLE & BARROW IN FURNESS

What a wonderful way to start a day! A shower without the usual noise and jostling of those waiting in a queue; room in which to dry myself and a bedroom all to myself. Breakfast is all that I could have wanted. I choose fresh grapefruit and herring in oatmeal, chosen last night from the comprehensive menu, plus fresh hot toast and preserves.

My host kindly takes me to the bus station for my bus at 10.50 for Carlisle. It is a welcome start to the day from my usual scramble for an early morning start.

Although I won't have long in Carlisle, a matter of two hours only I do discover what has made Carlisle famous care of the information leaflet picked up at the Tourist Office..

As a keen theatre goer, I am sure I would have been impressed at visiting Her Majesty's Theatre in 1880 when the theatre would have been lit by electricity: the very first in all England. As Humpty Dumpty would have said 'There's Glory for You'

We are now into more open countryside and veer off at Gretna Green, where in the past many a loving couple defied convention and their parents' wrath by speeding up north to be married secretly over Gretna's famous anvil. It still holds romantic associations with some couples, although the anvil is now a photographer's prop.

To my amusement a hitch hiker is thumbing a lift. Not your everyday hiker, but a fully kilted Scot with a plaid thrown over his shoulder and on his head a Tam O'shanter! We passed too quickly for me to see whether he had a set of bag pipes, however lucky is the driver that offers this man a lift. I can only hope that they understand each other's accents.

I have plenty of time to have a coffee, Chelsea bun and a loo stop at Carlisle station. Carlisle has many other famous and picturesque points including part of Hadrian's Wall defences, although this is one stop that I won't have time to look into its past.

Due to the awkwardness of road transport, or rather the supply of weekly volunteer drivers I have no alternative but to take the train to Barrow in Furness .for another connection to Lancaster. This will be more new country for me and I am looking forward to pastures new.

Just as I am collecting my kit, there is a train announcement.

The train at platform.... Is going all the way to Lancaster,.

A guard advises me to travel straight through rather than wait at Barrow for 1¾ hours for the next train. I decide to stay on the train and wait for Mike's arrival in Lancaster. There is no way that I can reach him at this late stage, as he would have set off and not realised that there is a change of plan as the train times will now differ.

It is obvious that we are in a different type of country, as the scenery changes to a more gentle character with more arable farming down this coast line.

This stretch of coast becomes ever closer and near Workington there is a row of shiny new turbine windmills in the sea; like some form of nymphs waving their arms encouraging sailors to join them on their bed of rolling foam. This is my first taste of wind turbines; and from a distance they do look rather delicate. I know that there will be hundreds more built both off shore and on land and they will take some getting used to. When I think that electricity pylons were put hither and thither over the countryside, there were complaints to every council and parliament. We got used to them, so in time we will get accustomed to the whirling of the turbines too.

It is now so different here, with the sun on the water, although I can see white crests of waves. I am pleased that I am on a 'coastal' trip and not confining myself to inland bus travel even with the occasional blips.

The train passes through Maryport and Workington, with several small unidentifiable villages and small housing settlements just tucked in off the coastal road.

We go through Whitehaven, now a bustling town which like most coastal towns started off as a small fishing community. Of course the Georgians and Victorians saw the potential and built well reflecting the prosperity from coal and iron. St Bees and its Nature Reserve is coming into view. Sandstone cliffs that tower to 500ft above the shore line house kittiwakes, fulmar and black guillemots as well as other nesting birds. It is believed that an Irish princess set up a nunnery here. It would have been well hidden, as it is in a wild secluded spot.

The tide is coming in and only patches of sand can be seen on my right. Our track is now only feet from the sea. Well, I wanted a coastal trip and this is not letting me down. This next stretch however has taken us over the sea. Or rather that the sea has come inland to meet us. We have sea on each side of the track. It is rather un-nerving, as the clouds are sneaking in with the turn of the tide, and I can't even see the shore, on either side! Were we afloat? This must be a lovely, long stretch of sand during high summer. As my worry about being over the water increases I look to landward and I have spotted an interesting tower inland with the hills in the background which look as if they have been 'painted by numbers'.

I have just seen Sellafield! It is monstrous. This is very reminiscent of The Quatermas Experiment television serial. It is both futuristic and alien with pipes and towers, tubes and belching steam. One could weave a whole science fiction story around it.. We hardly pause at Seascale although it must be a good spot for sailing, as I can see a dinghy or two fighting the waves. Ravenglass is much bigger altogether. Situated in a sheltered haven, it was the obvious area in which the Romans built a good sized fort on what must have been around 4 acres of land. The incoming sea now laps at the edges of the railway embankment as we cross the inlets and in some places there is tidal movement on both sides of the track. I would not fancy being on this journey if there was a fierce storm, that would be far too nerve shattering.

I'm sure that the names of some of the smaller town and villages that we pass en route stem from the Nordic: Annaside; Gutterby; Silecroft; Haverigg; are certainly not of modern origin. However Millom, now a drowsy place, but like most towns on this side of England is full of industrial history. A great iron mining community once thrived here, but as with other industries progress has taken over and now the town just holds on to a 14th century castle – now in ruins – and a 12th century church. Dalton in Furness also had its share of iron mining and walkers and casual visitors can be sure of seeing the remains.

We come inland now, nearly touching the A 595 and beyond the inlet I can see Morecambe Bay. The tide is out here exposing the miles of treacherous sand. Its appearance is not to be trusted however flat it looks, there are hidden pitfalls and quick sands here and strong incoming tides. It is possible to walk across the bay and at certain times a guide can take you across safely, which they have been doing so since around the 16th century. The railway now crosses over the top end of Morecambe Bay with sea water on either side of the elevated track as it heads for Arnside and the safety of dry land.

Now I've lost the sea as we head down to Lancaster. Our train is a little early, which gives me more time to have butterflies. It feels like a first date. Mike and I have been in contact more or less every day but now will be the first time in a fortnight that I'll have seen him – almost half way round and I find that I have missed him. I hope that he has missed me too.

Like a sensible fellow he has already booked us in for a night in a quiet farmhouse on the outskirts of the town which overlooks distant hills and has friendly cows leaning over the fence. I can now hand over all the excess luggage that I have carried around. Why I should think that a skirt and pretty top never mind the tape recorder, charger and a small library would stand me in good stead I have no idea. It will be good to have a proper bed, not to mention a good meal at the end of the day.

DAY 15 . WEDNESDAY 8TH JULY
LANCASTER TO CHESTER VIA BLACKPOOL, PRESTON AND SOUTHPORT.

After filling ourselves with a cooked breakfast, Mike puts me on the 0854 bus and hopes that we can meet me on time in Chester as he had affairs to attend to in the locality.

The bus trip feels very claustrophobic after my train journey and sea views. We pass through street after street of terrace houses and shops. Everything looks the same, with hardly any variation. I am depressed and sit with my nose in yet another book. Blackpool with its famous tower lifts me somewhat before I head for Preston and Southport. Southport is nice! It still has a feeling of gentility about it, anyone can see that although many shops will have changed use over the years, it still attracts the tourists. Its pier alone is worth a visit, at three quarters of a mile long, it has enough bracing sea air for anyone, and the little electric train that takes the stroller back is well worth the money. Situated as it does on the estuary, Southport mudflats plays host to hundreds, if not thousands of pink-footed geese, not to mention oyster-catchers and other seashore birds, while the dunes play a huge part in the lives of avid bird watchers.

It is nice to have a mini break on Lord Street to have coffee, stop at a bank and enjoy a leg stretch. Having had my schedule interrupted I have to get back on track and book several nights accommodation before heading for Chester.

As I check back on my time table I realise that I am nearly half way through my tour. The time is speeding by.

Chester is another 'first' for me. I knew something of its history, however with Mike as my guide it is something of a revelation. We walk what seems like several miles, along the medieval walls that ring the city. This city wall is the most complete circuit of Roman & medieval defensive town wall in Britain. This says something for the architects and the town council; not to mention all the people that have preserved it for the future. With a city so crammed full of interest, it will take more than one half day to absorb it. Eastgate, one of the more famous sites is built over the Roman east gate – naturally! Then in 1897 a clock was added to celebrate Queen Victoria's Diamond Jubilee. Of course there are a few Roman remains and Saxon fragments located around the city including the Bridge of Sighs linking the city jail to the chapel in Blue Coat Hospital where prisoners received their last rites. Like other bridges of that name, it derives from the moans and groans of the

criminals who went from prison to gallows. There must have been a lot of them passing over that bridge.

Poor King Charles stood on one of the towers in the wall, probably moaning too when he watched his army being defeated on Rowton Moor in 1645. I have put this city then on my 'places to visit' list. This list is lengthening daily and at this rate it will take the best part of a year to complete.

There is only one place that is a must, and that is 'The Row's.' A two tiered shopping complex, dating as far back as medieval through to Victorian times. Space was at a premium then too. We dined well on steak and chips and under £3. a piece. Even Mike was impressed. He is never one to spend excessively on dining out!

There was one downside to the day. Mike asked me how I had got on getting from Glasgow and whether I had enjoyed my time in Dumfries. I vented my feelings about bus station officials and the lack of buses when one was needed and that I hadn't really known where I was en route to Dumfries not having a map to hand. When I remarked on the fact that I thought Moffat was quaint he proceeded to take the wind out of my sails by telling me that my journey had been so far inland that I was in danger of reaching Carlisle before I had got to Dumfries! This was not what I wanted to hear. The whole trip had, to my mind been ruined by the reaction of a positively awkward person. I had missed the coast line entirely. Where words had failed me at the bus station, I sat in the car and used every swear word I knew and Mike, sensing my annoyance and frustration offered me a few more that he had picked up during his time in the forces. Then for good measure added some more that his father had gleaned from his time in the navy. I just had to get over it and press on but I was determined that that type of slip would NOT happen again come hell or high water!

He leaves me to confirm my overnight bookings as he and I part company at the bus station. Now I miss him as I go and locate my overnight hostel.

Into Wales

DAY 16. THURSDAY 9TH JULY
BANGOR VIA RHYL AND LLANDUDNO

I am glad that I have booked well ahead, as the summer season is approaching and bedding down for the night could be a problem especially as I am heading for 'tourism country' When I ring Perranporth hostel, the warden is very considerate of my well being and stresses that there will be a small group of partying girls staying there following their G.C.E's or A'levels. 'Will this be a problem?' he asks. At least he has given me the opportunity to change hostels or find other accommodation in time. I wonder if he thinks that I may not be able to understand the young? Or that I am too old to remember being that age. If only he knew what I got up to when I was 17 years of age, and I have no intention of letting Mike know either.

My connection in Rhyl, for once is well timed, as I have only 5 minutes to wait for the Llandudno bus.

The weather has now taken a turn for the worse. Rain clouds are scudding across and rain is in the air. I did not expect to see anybody on the sand until a small family group came in sight. A caravette is parked nearby and a woman and small children are huddled behind a wind breaker. Dad is cooking a meal on a grill. I could see that the wind was getting the better of the fire, as the smoke was swirling. This was the idea of a British holiday. Stoic, determined and everyone will jolly well like it attitude. I watched as long as I could, but Mum was rooted to the spot and would expect her late breakfast brought to her. I sincerely hoped that they would enjoy the rest of their stay! The seaside around Colwyn Bay and the small but pretty Rhos on Sea lead to Llandudno, rightly famous for the Great Orme the high limestone headland that dominates the town. If one is of a fit nature one can clamber, walk or stroll up to the top for a restorative cuppa. The other alternative is to take Britain's longest cable car or the funicular railway for the amazing views from the top.

I was a bit disappointed in Llandudno; perhaps I did not see it at its best. It was a dull day, the wind was keen, and there was rain filling the air in a steady drizzle. There was short flight of stairs to the Sandbach cafe, where I had a well filled sandwich and side salad that was a meal in itself. I felt then that I was brave enough to go and look at the sea.

It was many years since I was last here, way back in my childhood and too far back to recall anything in particular. Today there was only one solitary child on the small stretch of sand toying with a bucket and spade. The promenade has elderly couples walking for the good of their health who, with stiff upper lips, would enjoy it or die. As I saw earlier the British are a stoic lot!

I am heading for Bangor. Another new place; where I am going to make time to visit the Cathedral, I may not get another chance and by all accounts it is a must on any one's itinerary.

I won't have time to check whether the Bible Garden really does have every type of plant mentioned in the Bible but I will go in to the cathedral to absorb one of the greatest religious buildings in the land. The little pamphlet that I pick up in the foyer tells me that the Cathedral of St. Deinol was founded in the 13th century, also that the monk St. Deinol established a cell here then a small church. Such was his influence that Maelgwn, King of Gwynedd gave him the land and the church grew to become Britain's second cathedral, which was restored in the 19th.century and is now the oldest cathedral still in use in Britain. The interior could have been over fanciful and ornate, instead it is simple in design with three sets of seating facing each other. The 12 stages of the cross around the walls were very tastefully done and I was impressed by the Mostyn Christ, a C16th carved oak figure. It was altogether a peaceful place.

The hostel too is above average. I was so getting used to hunting lodges, new builds, cramped space and meagre meals that this evening's repast is more that adequate. The menu is super. Yes, even a selection to choose from, written up on the board. I phone home and go into raptures about the choice offered. Mike informs me that he is trying to cook himself something to eat and will I go and choose something and leave him peace? I have a three course dinner and choose a small packed lunch for the following day. Our room, larger than some I have had previously is well supplied with hanging space and hangers. What luxury! I am so used to dumping my clothes on the floor or chair with everyone else's, that I feel that I have come to heaven. We are provided with not only a duvet but a blanket as well. What it is to come to a 'foreign' country!

For once the lounge area is what it said on the packet; that is with comfortable settee's and arm chairs. This evening these are taken up with resting travellers, some even walkers, rather than those that travel with over large rucksacks and black bin liners. A conversation starts up about how one should travel lightly. One girl advocates using the laundrette where possible, either in the hostel or hunting down one in a town.

'Ah!' said another obviously well used to out of the way hostels. 'What happens when there aren't any? Do you walk alone? Think of the others in your group? You have to keep to civilisation if you want those sort of facilities.'

'There lies the drawback in or out of season walking or indeed walking away from all that is necessary for sweet smelling companionship.' A seasoned walker replies. He turns to another bronzed walker.

'You're on your own, how do you manage?'

The young man smiles and answers: 'I set off with just enough clothes to see me through the week, visit a charity shop and replace whatever I need.' This last remark reminds me of the long distance walker I met in Wick who travelled very lightly and did much the same thing.

That starts off a heated argument as to what he should do with the clothing he has just taken off and washed, hopefully in a hostel, and whether the charity shop would want his cast offs, or even how long he would have to walk to find another shop. This brings the conversation back to where it started; to walk from town to town or branch off into the wilderness and hope for the best. I never found out just where he was heading or indeed where he had been. But it was a novel idea with a change of scene and a change of clothing.

DAY 17. FRIDAY 10TH JULY
LLANBEDR VIA PORTHMADOC AND MINFFORDD

I have a good continental breakfast including yoghurt and fruit, with time afterwards to post yet more post cards before catching the 9.50 bus. I'm glad I checked the time as I now have more time to see yet another place which is new to me. It is surprising that there are still some unknown towns and cities that have passed me by over the years.

Porthmadoc has been newly washed it looks so clean and fresh. What a delightful place, although at this time of year it is starting to fill with tourists. I share my sandwich with a friendly robin, and we both keep a watchful eye on the seagulls, who by their eye and demeanour are the local bullies. Local museums are a must if you have the time, and the maritime museum here is no exception. Small though it may be it was a wealth of information about the area and is well stocked with paintings. Like most tourists I wanted to join the Ffestiniog Railway for a short run. What a joy! The station staff jump in and out of the train like jack in the boxes. An aura of organised chaos reigns. Either this is the start of the tourists season or the railway personnel are new as many of them seem to have forgotten things that are obviously important to the running of the railway like dusters and oil cans..

When I had enquired at the information office about visiting Portmeirion, the staff were adamant that there would not be time to visit this remarkable miscellany of buildings, the dream child of William Clough Ellis. I had watched some of the episodes of 'The Prisoner' and would have liked to have a real experience of the place, but, they said there was a three mile walk from Minffordd station. Foiled again! In fact it was only a ten minute walk away. Yet another place to add to the 'must visit diary'.

On route to the little station I find a post office and send off a book with a small token of a love spoon to my distant husband, a Welsh Tradition that was usually carved and given to a fiancés intended, however I am sure that he will appreciate the thought behind the deed.

I have two local elderly gentlemen for company on the platform, who with excess yesses in their speech 'Oh yess' tell me how things have changed. 'Yess indeed!' One lamented that now there were only two families left in his row of terraces, but that at least some of the younger ones that had moved in were not week-enders and were permanent residents 'Oh yess. Indeed!' The other reminds me that I have to ask the guard to stop the train at Llanbedr as it is a request halt rather than a proper station.

The three of us wave to the train driver and he pulls in obligingly so that we don't have to walk far for the doors. Now we've come inland a bit there is no view of the sea from the train, although the countryside is open and although the clouds are building up the view across from either side is well worth looking at. This must be a busy line as the carriage is full of men having the time of their lives and not adverse to a bit of back chat so that I almost missed the view of Harlech Castle high above the dunes

I do as suggested and asked to be dropped off at Llanbedr, it seems that not a lot of passengers require this station, as it is nowhere near anywhere else. Checking the time of the train the following day I discover that I have to be on the station a good half hour earlier than listed. I am also advised that I must wave early enough for the train driver to spot me and stop. There is no platform here just a level crossing and I can only hope that trains go slow enough in either direction so that I am not run down in the process of crossing the line.

It's a good three quarter mile walk to the hostel which will work up an appetite, however it is a lovely tree lined road past a stream in which unaccompanied children are paddling and having fun as in Enid Blyton's stories. The hostel backs to on rock strewn water but stands full square to the main street. The houses that line the road are of good Welsh stone and just down the road is a pub. It's all very rural and quite delightful.

I have a very pleasant room with just six beds, one being occupied by Muriel who is happy to join me for our evening meal. We are unpacking when a knock comes at the door. A very pretty girl of twenty or so comes in. She is all angles and legs with the biggest dark brown eyes and reminds me of a forest faun. 'Could you advise me?' she asks.

'Certainly if we can,' says Muriel. 'How can we help?'

She tells us her name is Aileen and she is preparing to go on a cycling tour across Southern Australia with friends later in the year.

'I'm worried that I won't be able to buy moisturiser or lipstick.' She says 'Do you think there will be any shops?'

Neither of us had given much thought to the purchase of probable 'essentials' in the outback but this is of great concern to Aileen. We give it our best thought and hopefully, after finding out the approximate route that she and her friends are going to undertake advise that she buys small packets or bottles and tops up during her trip. Lipstick might be a problem as no doubt it will soften and get unusable. Aileen was aghast as Muriel itemised the FEW things that Aileen ought to take. If only they could see inside my rucksack! She has other more questions of a personal nature and in this we cannot help as chemists will be a rarity. Whether we have helped at all remains to be seen. She leaves to join up with her friends andwe do not see her again that evening. We can only hope that she and her chums work out a better plan before they leave. Muriel and I spend a hilarious half hour discussing what we would take on an extended tour in inhospitable places of the world.

Most of the other rooms are taken by fourteen young boys, which is presumably a group booking. This does not bode well for later, as I have found that boys en masse are not given to quiet.

Whilst in the kitchen the warden appears and tells me that all coffees and teas have to be paid for at twenty pence each, and he will count the teaspoons used, (and no doubt the tea bags as well). He is that type of warden who obviously has come across teaspoon thieves. At quite a number of hostels I had discovered that the teaspoons have to be pounced on or else they disappear without trace. He also informs me that breakfast is at half past eight, which is absolutely no good to me as my train leaves before twenty past. This will be a nuisance apart from anything else. Will I be able to have a coffee then? 'No', he says; 'The cupboards will be locked'. It is a good thing that I can use my own makings. I feel that things could have been arranged a bit better or even on a more friendly footing. This is the first time that I am required to wash up after a meal and put things away following our supper. I notice that the boys disappear smartly straight after they have eaten.

As the pub is open and feeling sociable I thought I would like to sample the local ale. As I'm deciding which pump to try a very hospitable local gent offers to treat me. Disappointed to find that there isn't a local beer but I am drinking a beer brewed in Stockport. We chat for some time about hostels in general and of a warden decades ago in some remote hostel who carried provisions for his hostel on his back for three hours as there was no vehicular access. I dread to think what would have happened if he couldn't make it in the days before mobile phones if he needed help. I excuse myself as I am tired and I have an early start. An hour lolling in a sofa of large and squashy proportions and doubtful antiquity I find that I am falling asleep. Muriel says she will wait for the news, but I am asleep before she comes up

I had a feeling those boys would make their presence felt! At around midnight the whole group start singing and banging doors. Just as they quieten down a bit; there is a knocking on our door and an unknown woman, (is she the warden's wife?) wakes me up to ask if we are in charge of this 'influx' ? as she calls it. Not content with waking me up she proceeds down the corridor and wakes up several other people to ask the same question. I cannot raise the enthusiasm to open our door again and find out what the response was to the question as Muriel has slept throughout the interchange. This whole episode gives me a headache and I have to rummage through my rucksack to locate Paracetamol and juice. I am not looking forward to getting up at the crack of dawn.

DAYS 18 & 19. SATURDAY 11TH & 12TH JULY
TENBY VIA MACHYNLLETH, ABERYSTWYTH, CARDIGAN AND HAVERFORDWEST

As I thought, morning has broken and my head feels like an empty drum. I find that I have only have access to the kettle with just enough time for a swift cup of coffee This is one of the moments when I am glad to have packed coffee, dried milk and sweeteners. As the warden is having a lie in or has been done away with by the group of yobs he has not unlocked the door so I to open a back window which fortunately is a casement type and climb out. Perhaps he will suspect the boys and not think that I have taken any of his precious teaspoons.

It is a bit un-nerving to stand on a level crossing and hope that the train driver is going to stop. However all is well and I am soon on my way.

I am back to following the shore once again. The sea is green and crashes on boulders at the edge of the breakwater. Would diesel trains have braved the heavy seas, I wonder? Barmouth opens up and I can see what a wonderful holiday spot this would be in high summer. The sand is more or less empty of holiday makers. There is a lone man and his dog striding across the expanse. The train goes steadily over a bridge above the incoming sea. The coast line is undulating with sand and tide mingling with each other. I can spot some small buildings nestling under grassy sand dunes. I am adding Barmouth to my ever increasing list to places to visit. At this rate I shall need another life time. This is such a wonderful natural place for a holiday, with no apparent 'kiss me quick' hats or the trappings of the up-market all singing, all dancing resort. The only ingredient missing is sunshine. We go through Fairbourne with its concrete breakwater, which resembles 'sandcastles' Now this stretch between Fairbourne and Llwyngwrl is an eye opener as the sea is fifty or so feet directly below us. There doesn't seem to be anything holding us up. What happened to the track? As the train slowly curves I try and check for erosion. Being coastal is one thing, being sea borne is another. It is quite extraordinary and in a way surreal. I just wish that I had been warned that we would be afloat.

We now come across a caravanserai of caravans. I am sure that this is the name for such a collection. Row upon row of caravans and chalets line the bay's grey muddy shingle. What a contrast! A mini-town, after the peace and space of the last half hour the difference is marked.

Another wind break, another family and camper van with extension in the middle of no-where. They must have a good imagination to think that they are on the Costa Del Sol and not fifty yards or so from the rest of humanity.

We are coming into low cloud now and the view is obscured and as I reach further inland for my train at Machynlleth it starts to rain. I have been lucky so far. Only at John O'Groats did I encounter heavy rain, plus a heavy drizzle in Llanbedr, so I count myself fortunate.

The station is empty save for the queue at the ticket office where several people require tickets for trains which do not run on Saturdays. They, like me, find time-tables a mystery. Finding that I am not the flavour of the month as I know where I am going when I buy my ticket, the other passengers 'draw their skirts aside' and glare at me. I feel that I am being totally shunned as I sneak into my seat and pretend that I am not there while looking out of the window at the rain soaked landscape. There is nothing to see except wet roof tops, as shiny as seals. This is another time when I am glad that I have a book in my rucksack.

As I leave the train at Aberystwyth I try to ring the tourist information office but the signal on my phone is too low. This is inconvenient to say the least as I need to book two nights accommodation at a B & B in Tenby as this has been timetabled.

I have now to change back to buses this afternoon and find myself dodging holiday makers who are impervious to the weather – it is raining hard - people are dashing about in T shirts and shorts but with umbrellas. Overheard conversation as to whether the weather will worsen is non-stop. I now expect a tornado at the very least. The café provides me with not just a super sandwich but an interesting table companion who asks me if I know Abersytwyth at all well?

I reply that my knowledge of the sea side resort is limited, as I haven't visited since my childhood with my mother. I feel that I am going to be regaled by a long history of the town. Fortunately the gentleman just tells me that he is proud that the Welsh Language Society, Cymdeithas yr Iaith, has it headquarters here.

'I didn't know that' I replied, assuming that it would have been further north instead.

'There's a interesting story as to that' He goes on. 'A member of the society was going home on a bicycle along the front, with his girl friend on the back holding on tight. Unfortunately the person who stopped him was a policeman and the cyclist was given a summons.'

I felt that there was more to come.

'Oh yes' he went on. 'The cyclist ignored that summons – Why? Because it was in English you see'

'Ah! I understand now. No doubt that would have set the cat among the pigeons?

' I replied with a smile.

'Oh yes, others joined in the rebellion and refused to pay fines because all the paper work was in English and our language was dying out. It stirred up quiet a hornets nest. That's why you now see all the place-names and road signs in two languages.'

'Quite right too' I remark.

We separate on good terms and I say thank you to him in my best Welsh.

Lunch over I try calling the tourist office from a phone box (my batteries being a bit low I expect that this will be a long conversation.) when I ask for a single room they are insistent that single rooms at this time of year are as rare as the sunshine. No doubt I would find this humorous if my night's sleep didn't depend on finding a room, any room somewhere. With a lot of patience – on my part – the office gives me six numbers to try. The first two are un-obtainable, the next can't oblige and gives me an alternative number (just in case!) Now I've run out of both time and money! I'll have to try my luck later and hope for the best.

Yet another change in Cardigan, more rain and more disgruntled passengers. When the weather is poor the spirits are low, nobody wishes to talk and the thoughts of home and fireside loom large. Also I am getting worried about my sleeping arrangements and I can only hope that one of my numbers comes up trumps. My finances do not run to top quality hotels, even if that were available in Tenby at this time of year. I am certainly not the best dressed for such a hotel either. I try my luck again on my mobile but with no luck as the battery is now virtually dead.

This whole exchange has made me run for the bus and I am thankful that it is warm, so warm indeed that I am on the point of sleep when the buses reverses abruptly into a turn around area in what seems the middle of the country. Have we broken down? There is no explanation as we are all hurried off and bundled into another Richard Bros. bus for Haverfordwest. The passengers and myself had not been told of this exchange and we weren't told whether in fact there was a fault with the bus or it was the end of the driver's shift. Most perplexing! I am not fully wide awake to recognise any of Haverfordwest, which is a pity as a child I spent many happy hours here and in Milford Haven with family.

Whether the day feels unduly long or the number of buses has confused me or

I am just worried that time is running out. I find a phone box and start dialling. Three phone calls later and a Mrs Edwards answers the phone. She sounds very cheerful when I ask about a single room for two nights. Yes she can put me up; as long as I don't mind that it is a small room reserved for family and there is no en-suite?

I am so cock-a –hoop that the price isn't referred to.

I am glad that I made the call when I did, as the Tenby bus is early and I arrive in good time, to be greeted by Mrs Edwards, who invites me to a cuppa before I have taken my coat off. There are more apologies for the room – In reality I suspect that this is her room I have taken.

On retiring I find, by opening the wrong door, that in fact kind Mrs Edward, is sleeping in what I would refer to as the airing cupboard on the landing. Thank you Mrs. Edwards for going to such trouble on my behalf; it was much appreciated.

There is an Australian couple staying here and they heartily recommend a restaurant overlooking the harbour. Mike has stayed in Tenby long, long ago and has recommended the same place namely The Plantagenet Restaurant.

Showered and in my right mind I too enjoy the view at sunset overlooking the harbour before having a quiet and restful evening catching up on all the local news via the Australian couple.

What bliss! waking up in a proper bed; albeit with the seagulls having a committee meeting right outside my window. My digestive system has been at sixes and sevens since I started, what with having to buy what ever I could carry or rely on what the hostels had to offer. Then when good food was offered I took my fill and now realise that I have been suffering from a lack of fruit and greens. So I refused the full English breakfast and filled up on fruit and yoghurt.

Tenby has a lovely stretch of sand and interesting rocks and pools which I now will have time to explore; I had hoped that I could wander through Tenby's winding maze of streets; however there is only one drawback. The wind and rain have worsened, and I can see from my vantage point of the bay window that determined holiday makers are scuttling from shop to café and back to their car or hotel. I did so want to laze the day away on the beach! Like other Britons with their best gung ho attitude, I make up my mind to join them so venture forth to brave the elements, look at the sea, and like the other holiday makers dive into a café and fortify myself with a coffee. Back at Mrs. Edwards' I spend an hour writing up my notes from the previous day and luckily just as I am finishing the rain ceases at one thirty, just in time for lunch back at the Plantagenet Restaurant where I settle for a child's size portion of the lamb. Perhaps my order was lost in translation but the plate is overflowing. What would an adult's portion consist of; and how big would the plate have to be?

The streets are as topsy turvey as I remembered from my childhood and I spend a delightful hour exploring the twists and turns, popping into those little souvenir shops that refuse to close on a Sunday. St. Mary's Church is having a flower festival this weekend. What a joy! I love decorated churches, and this is no exception. The displays are down both sides of the church and I am pleased and delighted to see that this year's theme has a hymn motif. Some of the unlabelled displays are well known hymns which are easy to identify while other hymns which must

be popular at this church are difficult to work out. But all are so colourful and imaginative. Realising that I have been there for over an hour and that evensong is only twenty or so minutes away I rest among the flowers and I am at peace with the world and the air is filled with perfume. The service is conducted by Rector Jenkins who obviously is very well thought of as is demonstrated afterwards by the parishioners. The final hymn is 'Now the Day is Over' nearly brings me to tears, as this was the last thing my class sang every Friday in my infant school back in Swansea. Suddenly I am back there, with sunny afternoons and the air filled with dust motes and the day is over and I head for home. That reminiscing was the last thing I would have thought of. I leave a bit sad. I jolly myself up with tea at Blueberry's and I spend the evening watching My Fair Lady on the television.

DAY 20. SUNDAY 13TH JULY
BATH VIA SWANSEA AND BRISTOL

The seagull committee wakes me at some ungodly hour and in consequence I have showered and packed my rucksack before breakfast. As I leave I thank Mrs. Edwards profusely for her hospitality and kindness. This next stretch will be a reasonably short journey only passing through both Swansea and Bristol before my next destination.

Checking the time table, time seems a little short for the change over in Bristol, so being very on the ball I purchase a sandwich for lunch.

As we reach the environs of Swansea I feel quite disorientated. Bearing in mind that I haven't visited my home town since 1966 it's not to be wondered at. I find it sad that a place that I knew well is now just a distant memory. The only thing that I can recall is that Adelina Patti sang there and that the Patti Pavilion in the Victoria Park was named after her. Mother and I used to go there quite often and walk round what was known as the 'Winter Gardens' The other thing that comes to my mind was that the largest telescope in Wales was on the beach, although for the life of me I can't now visualise it. I also recall that mother and I were excited at hearing the cricket spectators in the cricket pavilion at the same time as hearing it on a wireless from one of the houses. It was all amazing then, so very remarkable to my mother who grew up with her father making a 'cat's whisker' wireless. One of my earliest memories of living there is the Mumbles pier and thinking how wonderful it was to walk over the sea. Opposite the entrance to the pier was a small cinema; It has probably been pulled down years ago. This was where my mother and I saw an early 3D film. At that time everyone was issued with paper glasses, with one red and one green lens. Now this I DO remember. First there was a plate of eggs bacon and chips shown on the screen; then a hand came holding a bottle of tomato ketchup and commenced to pour it over the food. The bottle continued to pour and pour, filling the plate and the screen. Naturally there were loud intakes of breath and people ducked to get away from the ketchup. When that finished we were treated to a lady in a off the shoulder black evening dress who poured red wine into a glass. Of course the wine flowed over the glass and onto the screen. Again everyone ducked and put their hands to their heads. Life was simpler, even 'naïve' then. But it was something I'll never forget. Not that I can say what film it was, or indeed if it was just an experiment.

I spend the rest of the journey looking for places that I recognise as we reach Bristol. Either there has been a total re-building of the city or we have entered by the 'tradesman's entrance' so to speak. I don't recognise any of it. I'm glad I thought of the sandwich for lunch as the connection in Bristol for Bath is reduced to a mere five minutes.

Bath bus station is full of noisy people and I stand in a queue for half an hour checking my destination, ticket and finding the bus to the hostel. It's times like this that patience is a virtue! The wait was worth it, as the bus drops me off outside the gate to the hostel's drive. This hostel is very impressive indeed. It is a square 'Italianate' building with an incredible façade, mini turrets and many windows. The place is awash with American and Australian tourists who are galloping around Europe as if they are just going on a brief jaunt. My five week sojourn seems tamer by the minute, and I don't intend to mention it to anyone in case they consider that I am just on an afternoon's stroll.

The lounge is well stocked with incredibly comfortable chairs in which are quickly occupied. At reception I am agreeably surprised to be supplied with crisp white sheets instead of a cotton sleeping bag, which can cause some distress as well as amusement. Whilst washing out socks and T shirt a member of staff watching me offers very kindly to spin dry my things along with his own items. Gratefully I accept this and hope that I can remember to collect these before I leave in the morning.

There is only the one disadvantage to meeting up with international travellers who are spending a year living from a suitcase or in their case rucksacks as their rucksacks tend to be three feet tall and weigh as much as a person: plus these Amazons carry as least one black plastic bag full of who-knows-what which when nudged or kicked in the dark have a tendency to move across the floor and get in the way. Roz, whom I met in Tongue, had the right idea when she said a ruck-sack full of draw string cloth bags for different items was the ideal baggage solution.

DAY 21. MONDAY 14TH JULY
ILFRACOMBE VIA BARNSTAPLE, BIDEFORD AND BUDE

I find that during the night others have come to bed and deposited their overstuffed bin liners around the floor; so it is with great perseverance that I have to forage between them and their carrier bags to locate my wash kit. What were they doing during the late evening? They could have hardly been shopping, as there were no carriers in the room when I went to bed. Judging by the size and density of them there is a dead body in there somewhere. I do remember to collect my laundry which, bless the man, has been folded neatly and left on top of the drier.

I make what I can out of breakfast and run into a problem. There is no kettle! Why is there no kettle? I have just put on a saucepan to boil water when a young girl comes into the kitchen with it. With neither explanation nor apology.

On checking my time table I am over the moon at having at least a full hour before catching my next bus and can explore parts of Bath.

The Pump Room is my first stop and I can only take a peep through doors and railings, as I feel the entrance fee of £6 is a little high to go and dip my toe in bath water, even if I would be allowed. So I content myself visualising what it must have been like when Romans took their ease in the pool. Would they have had mixed bathing? They could be quite an open minded lot. Or were their 'ladies only' days?

Of course there is a lot more to Bath and bathing: There are Bath Oliver biscuits, of which my husband is very fond. These were taken after drinking the waters of Bath, presumably to take away the taste. There are Bath chairs and Bath buns; and I'm sure that there are many other things connected with Bath. By accident I came across the house that once belonged to Sally Lunn, who made the famous Sally Lunn Cakes. I would have dearly liked to have taken a peep inside as it was still a cake shop. Unfortunately it was closed. Wouldn't it have been wonderful if some of the original fixtures and fittings were still in place? I just had to make enquiries about this famous lady. I only have faded memories of ever eating a Sally Lunn cake. The building alone is dated 1680 which must make it one of Bath's oldest buildings. Then I discovered that Sally Lunn was in fact a Huguenot immigrant who made her name making these 'brioche' style buns, which would have given her fond recollections of France. It would have been fantastic to have tried a Sally Lunn bun or even taken tea in 'her' restaurant.

For once my mode of transport is late and I wait patiently with others for the train to take me back to Bristol and then onward to Bridgewater.

We go through Nailsea and Yatton with its handsome Railway Inn, built in stone and very imposing it is. Rows of neat houses, also stone built, and looking for all the world like a child's Lego construction Now whether it is that I am reaching saturation point or that I am just not used to carrying my worldly goods around on my back like a turtle but my right foot is aching. Perhaps I am just walking oddly but I feel as if Bridgewater bus station has doubled its size. I find a seat where I rearrange my rucksack, switch my overnight bag to the other shoulder and go in search of someone to ask the location of the bus stop.

The journey to Minehead passes through deliciously sounding places. Nether Stowey and Stoke Coursey. What luck! I am sitting on the right side of the bus to see the church with its verdigris copper spire. I could have so easily missed that.

I change buses once again in Watchet, which in its hey day must have been a lively place to live as an elderly lady at the bus stop tells me how she used to go dancing and whooping it up here. Not only did Watchet have a ballroom but it had a cinema! They must have had a lot of fun in Watchet. She said that this of course was when she was a lot younger. By the smile on her face I can see she had a good time. We motor on through pretty Cambwich with lanes only just wide enough for the bus. I dread to think what would happen if we come upon anything wider then a push bike. Mothers with push chairs just wouldn't stand a chance.

We creep down the lanes and pass Dunster Castle when I spot a sign for Dunster Doll Museum. There are signs also for the West Somerset Railway on my right. We are into pretty and quaint, picturesque and photogenic now. Pass the church of St. Peter, formerly a salt store, and we are in picture postcard Porlock, which is bathed in afternoon sunshine. Whitewashed cottages and shops flank the main street. There are boats bobbing in 17th century Porlock Weir which has large lock gates once used to control the water level in the harbour. Porlock is enchanting, another place for my 'visit again' list.

We now have nail-biting hair pin bends to contend with. High bracken hedges on either side of the bus with occasional glimpses of rolling downs which can be seen between the foxgloves. The bracken gives way to gorse clumps, heather and bilberry. The sun has gone in and a horse and rider gallops over the moorland; could this be John Rudd or his love 'Lorna Doone?' It is the right countryside for it. We are climbing all the time and the bottom edges of clouds are only 100 feet or so above us. This is the country of highwaymen and secret assignations, sheep rustlers and horse and cart – not modern day madness.

Suddenly the sea is far below us and only short peeps can be seen as the hedgerow blocks my vision. The sea is now in front of us; how the lane twists and turns. We go past Contisbury church and the Sandpiper Inn, creep past cars having to back into hedges, the drivers are obviously on holiday as locals would be more pragmatic and not sit muttering curses at us. We are heading for Lynton and Lynmouth, the scene of a disaster in the 1950's when the flood waters of the Lynn River tore down the gorge and through the two towns. At the moment it's nestling drowsily in the afternoon sun. No visible remnants are now of the flood damage remain. We are steadily climbing again and are nearly touching the tree tops, the road is so steep here all the way up to Lynbridge and the Lynton and Lynmouth Tourist Information Office. This is a picturesque building, almost Tyrolean in style; all set about with flower bedecked balconies. There are even two towers.

We pick up several passengers here including a gentleman in a fawn pac-a-mac, who is followed by his wife, in a white pac-a-mac. She is also sporting a mauve woolly crocheted pull on hat, with tufts of hair escaping through the holes.

They sit behind me.

For the next hour the lady points out the obvious to her husband in a slow monotone.

'Oh look! The sun has come out now.'

'We might be turning left here, or we might be turning right'.

'If we had missed this bus we would have had to have caught the next one.'

'That's a big tree, the tree in our garden isn't as tall as that.'

There were other passing observations, about houses, the sky, and the landscape. In between these enlightening remarks she hummed tunelessly.

Passengers were trying not to smile indeed some were looking a mite worried. The lady's voice was of the piercing kind.

I tried to focus on the view around me. We are kissing ivy clad trees and walls, so near that twigs and leaves were being brushed off. There are signs of colour in the walls. Summer is on its way. We drop down a gear to enter Coombe Martin and rattle through the streets as our bus has become 'out of service.'

'Hangman's Hill' now overlooks the bay. Who was hung here and why? What did he or they do? Probably, in this neck of the woods, smuggling would be the answer.

The lady behind is still mentioning what is around us, somewhat to the amusement of the other passengers.

Then it came to me! He must be partially sighted and she his 'eyes.' This is why he hasn't spoken in all this time. What an inconsiderate fool I am. I figuratively slap my wrist.

Then suddenly he speaks! He is sure that the man in the field was the man that they saw that same morning.

'No' says his wife. 'The one we saw that morning had a green hat on not a yellow one.'

'Ah!' he replies 'You're right! The morning man did wear a green hat and if that isn't the morning man because the morning man wore a green hat not the yellow hat he is wearing now then probably it is a different man all together!'

Fortunately for the sanity of the rest of the passengers the couple got off the bus at the next stop. I, like the rest just couldn't stop giggling for a long time.

The bus station at Ilfracombe was down near the harbour, with no directional signpost pointing to the hostel. I am told to look skywards. Great heavens I must climb diagonally up a steep slope and umpteen steps to reach it! When I do arrive it is too late to book my evening meal, which should have been ordered before 6pm. This is not what I want at the end of the day. Then comes another shock when I am shown my sleeping arrangements. It is the top bunk in a room that contains three sets of bunks and hardly any floor space. My night time trip to the loo is not going to be a happy one.

Having had a very light lunch in anticipation of a good evening meal, hunger forces me to search out food. I have little choice at this time of the day and have to content myself with a pizza from a take-away whilst sitting on a rock watching the tide at a distance. Somewhere out there is the Chapel of St. Nicholas, on Lantern Hill, still burning a light for sailors as it did in the thirteen hundreds.

The ladder to my bunk nearly defeats me and I ponder on the likelihood of throwing myself on the mercy of the warden and ask if I can share their room. But after being refused a meal this notion slips away. There isn't room on the floor for me to curl up with pillow and duvet, as the entire area is taken up with my room mates clothing and belongings.

As I feared; my night time trip to the toilet is fraught. In the process of using the opposite top bunk as a first step, the occupant turns over in her sleep and I nearly step on her. Now I have to turn round and slide off the bunk, catching my shins on the rungs of the ladder. I have known better and more comfortable sleeping arrangements.

DAY 22. TUESDAY 15TH JULY
BOSCASTLE VIA BARNSTAPLE, BIDEFORD AND BUDE

I am thankful that I can catch an earlier bus from the high street, as my time at Ilfracombe hostel has not really been at the top of my list.

The stretch between Barnstaple; once the ancient capital of North Devon, and Bideford is a picture, with distant rolling hills emerging between the hedgerows.

We pass squat houses and farms and a sign pointing to Tapeley Park.

Some of the villages and hamlets must have their names derived from some farm or farmer or perhaps the crop or livestock. They might even have come from a well known personage or eccentric!

We slip down to Derriton, it's more inland than I really wanted, but I cannot divert the bus route, no matter how much I would like to. However the switch back and sharp bends that cause chaos amongst other road users more than make up in excitement for this 'detour.' A lady passenger who is sitting opposite me leans across and asks if I had heard of the 'socialite' collie?

'No I haven't' I replied

Apparently there is a passing place for buses, where the drivers would pause and exchange news. This young dog, watching from a garden wall would wait for the bus to pull up and climb aboard while it was stationary and the door was opened. When the drivers had finished their conversation the door would be opened again and the dog would jump out and wait for the next bus. It didn't seem to want to travel anywhere. It just liked sitting for a while on a bus. We pondered over this and she put forward a suggestion that the dog was in training for reconnaissance work for the C.I.A.!

You can never tell what fellow travellers will come up with!

I have to change at Barnstaple for Bideford with its steep winding narrow medieval streets, some with interesting names; Homestone and Gunstone, leading down to the quay. These must have meant something back in Elizabethan times. Then enough time to buy a sandwich and a carton of juice and call at the obligatory loo.

As we near Bude I am astonished at the height of the honeysuckle filled hedges; these must be all of ten feet high. Of course I realise that in fact the 'hedges' are stone banks across which foliage and flowers had taken root and flourished. I feel as if we are motoring down a 'fairy glen'. Some of the hedges are slightly overgrown patiently waiting for the hedge trimmer to come and give them a short back and sides.

We pass the turn off for Dizzard and Dizzard Point. Now those are place names to conjure with.

The steep run down to Crackington Haven makes the teeth clench, those who manage to keep their eyes open and not pray can see the boulder and rock strewn beach directly ahead. Forget the theme parks and the roller coasters. Just pay your two pound odd bus fare and sit gripping your hands and you should have a whale of a time and you actually get somewhere. When we arrive more or less in one piece I notice Coombe Barton Inn. Clever planning! Those that survive the run down will surely take full advantage of the odd pint or two here. The roller coaster ride hadn't quite finished as we twist our way up towards Brockhill Methodist Church. Those penitents who survived walking up would be captivated by the view in all directions. It is spectacular! Any preacher would have to be good to hold their congregation's attention.

The hedges close in one again and are a mass of foxglove, rose, campion, daisies and snapdragon. I hope that the dreaded hedge trimmer doesn't get here until the flowering season is over.

I arrive thankfully in Boscastle at one forty five. It is quite a novel experience to have nearly a full half day to explore. Boscastle is very, very attractive. A bubbling river flows down from the hill. Either side a collection of houses and shops; mainly to take money from the tourist. But I can see that it is also a town for the residents too. A cafe catches my eye and in a mad moment I order a Cornish pasty and a beer. Perhaps I should have checked on how many this pasty would have fed before I started on it. It was of a size that a family of four would have left crumbs. I did the best I could with it but having had most of my days taken up with sitting I really shouldn't have taken on such a monster.

Having had hiccups in the past about transport times I check my bus for tomorrow. As I suspected the times deviate from my list so carefully prepared beforehand.

The Museum of Witchcraft looks tempting and I don't wish to book in to the hostel until needs be so I pay my money and enter. What I was expecting I'm not sure, perhaps pixies, fairies and local folk lore. This museum is not for the faint hearted. By the time I had gone less than half way round I was singing hymns under my breath, including 'I love my Lord Jesus above everything'. As well as saying a little prayer or two. I chatted with the owner when I came out. A strange man, who had built the museum up over several years, he said that there were people who where fascinated by it and others who it frightened half to death. (I was one of the latter) He himself had death threats in the past and dead animals left on the doorstep.

I needed to fortify myself with a good old fashioned ice cream. Never mind the indigestion.

The hostel is situated behind the souvenir shop which looks like a fairy cottage, all surrounded by flowers and is sparklingly white. Miraculously, just at that moment, there aren't any visitors standing in front of the shop nor any cars. This is definitely the moment for a snapshot. I can just see an inch or two of the hostel behind the shop with its green triangle of the Y.H.A. sign a little behind. The hostel has, at one time, been home to the horses which pulled up the rowing boats, previously used to manoeuvre ships which were too large to enter the narrowing entrance to the harbour without assistance.

After leaving my belongings and signing in I am in desperate need of a leg stretch and cross the river, at this time of the year more of a broad shallow stream, I head towards the sea, clambering over rocks towards the harbour.

It is very calming sitting there, looking out to sea. Waves roll gently over the rocks then rustle and splash their way back. From this point I can't see the village

at all tucked away as I am in my little nook.

Post cards and stamps have to be bought, which means a stroll back into the village where the elderly shop assistant has difficulty in working out the price of five stamps at twenty pence each. Visitors are now filling the streets, and ice creams are being eaten in large quantities. Can a small child really consume a double portion of ice cream with clotted cream and a chocolate flake?

The hostel is open and airy, with long tables set down each side and a large one in the middle. Linda, the part time warden, is a farmer's wife. No doubt her husband is doing double duty while she is tending to us. We are treated to chicken casserole and, no doubt, home grown vegetables and encouraged to partake of home made elderflower cordial. This is home from home! We sit at the long tables like a school dinner hall and everyone has a holiday feeling about them and talks about their time in Devon. That is until it starts raining. There had been some mention of most of us walking to the village pub, but the hostel is too cosy and the company too good while the rain is worse. So there we all sit like a class of children at a boarding school writing letters and post cards home. On the walls are early photos of floods in the harbour which show just what damage the water can do; not to mention the heavy snow that can fall in the area.

The hostel had had a make-over in the last few years when the dormitories had been upgraded. One side of the hostel being set out for men, and the other for women.

We girls were under the eaves, with low mattresses either side of the room. Each bed had its own wall lights and the beams held our towels nicely to dry over night.

The warden books accommodation and food for me at Cosham some days off.

DAY 23. WEDNESDAY 16TH JULY
PERRANPORTH VIA WADEBRIDGE, PADSTOW AND NEWQUAY.

There are early risers this morning, some even starting out at 6.30. The rest of us have a leisurely breakfast; farmhouse style – including home made jams and marmalade. How does the warden have the time? Bless her heart she also packs up sandwiches for me and a small cake (home made – of course) and

slips a little post card into my packet. There is another late starter, by accident rather than design, doing a gap year and working her way round Europe from New Zealand. Tracy is also heavily laden as she has artist's materials in her back pack and intends to paint the views as well as photograph them. I give Tracy our address and she promises to visit in a few months time when she is in our area.

We spend the bus journey watching out for old Cornish tin mines on the distant hills. She is thrilled when she finally spots one, as some of her fellow travellers have told her all about the mines and the working conditions.

Tracy leaves me at Camelford and I go on to Wadebridge where I change for Padstowe. Here I am surprised that such a small fishing harbour can take this amount of tourists, especially as there is a large collection of push bikes leaning on the harbour wall. Is it a rally, or a race? There are no cyclists about, and nobody seems to be concerned about the dozen or so bikes. One museum is closed, but a souvenir shop is open plus many cafes offering local delicacies, most likely fish dishes, on their menus. Padstowe being famous for fish restaurants have queues a mile long. I couldn't locate the Information Office. Naturally everyone I ask doesn't live within fifty miles if they speak English at all. I really need to stock up on disposable undies and find a small chemist shop which charges me over the odds. An artist has set out his canvas and easel at the harbour wall, His eye has been caught by the complexity of the rigging on a yacht which is moored in the harbour. He has done some preliminary sketches, although at the moment he is filling his canvas with sky but the movement of the clouds and shades of blue is making this difficult. He and his canvas plus the scenery is so photogenic that I have to capture him on my camera.

There is no earlier bus to Newquay, perhaps my timing is wrong? How I wish I had gone right through from Wadebridge. Ah well! Like so many of the holiday makers I too use the harbour wall as my table and un-wrap my sandwiches with, as I suspected, a home made flapjack all neatly wrapped up in a paper napkin. The sweet post card Linda has included has a picture of two people in wet weather gear walking in the rain with a caption that reads 'Some people do it for fun' On the back she has written 'Happy munching, LINDA'.

I will have happy memories of Linda and her cooking. That is what home from home hostelling is all about. The welcome, the good cooking plus excellent overnight accommodation. Linda was a marvel, looking after twenty five people, while she and her husband ran, I am sure successfully, a farm nearby.

The bus ride to Newquay is nail-biting. 'Suicide Alley' is well known to drivers of both buses and the locals. It is frighteningly narrow, with more than a few hair pin bends. Visiting car owners cower and shiver in the hedgerows as we pass. One or two look scared stiff. The holiday brochures obviously didn't warn them about this aspect of Cornwall. The locals, who are easily spotted, either overtake each other - never mind the consequences of scraped paint work - or reverse confidently into gateways to let us proceed.

There are several small and attractive bays which, at the moment, are virtually deserted. The whole of this coast is ruled by the sun; if there isn't any sun, no-one knows what to do with themselves if it isn't sunny.

The sun briefly comes out as we reach Perranporth which allows me to see the wide expanse of sand curving round in a wide sweep. I am on the hunt for individual portions of food once again. Carrying cartons of fresh milk is always a problem with a surplus after my two or three cups of coffee for which other hostellers will no doubt thank me when I have left. I feel virtuous as I choose a banana and other fruit, although I had been assured that I will be well fed. I am fully aware that this is the hostel which will have riotous teenagers, out until all hours and singing their way to bed hugging tinnies and trannies. Will I get any sleep? Should I have looked for other accommodation?

There is a long up hill walk to the hostel, across a field following a track and over a stile. If any teens manage to walk up here after a night out they will hopefully be sober as a judge before they have reached the gate. Hot and weary I approach the garden where three pretty girls are sunning themselves on a bench. They smile and say 'Hi' These do not look like I imagined, They do not have a wild look in their eye and offer me a can of coke and say that I can leave my rucksack in the hall as I have half an hour to wait before the hostel officially opens its doors.

They are six girls in total, all who have just finished a full month's G.C.S.E. exams and are here for a relaxing week's break. When I ask when the party is about to start, they look bewildered and find the question funny. No; no partying, no heavy drinking, no high jinks, just girls relaxing. I'm not sure whether I feel let down as I was getting in the mood for a midnight feast at the very least. Ah well! Partying is not perhaps advisable at my age, who knows where I might lead them?

The warden, John, to my amusement, acts in loco parentis after the evening meal, he stresses that the girls return back to the hostel in good time from their evening out (Is there a curfew?) and to remember which bed they are sleeping in. This to my mind can be taken two ways! Don't forget, he says as they are leaving that they must behave themselves. The hostel has a quasi-family feeling, especially as he calls everyone by their first name. At the dining table there sits a family of four. Mum, Dad and two children. Those two made more noise and rumpus than all the girls put together. They rush up and down the room and are excessively noisy. All I can hope is that they are sleeping far away from me. After my time at Llanbedre I am wary about small children during the night hours.

Bless their hearts: three of the girls are back in their beds by 11pm (There are four of us in one room) They all whisper and tip toe as they get undressed and I haven't the heart to say that I have lain awake. The other three are sleeping further down the corridor and have broken their curfew despite John's warning and entered via a window and talked until at 4am.

I can only thank my lucky stars that the three that I had were the sweetest things.

The Bottom Bit

DAY 24. THURSDAY 17TH JULY

PENZANCE VIA ST. IVES AND LAND'S END

Over breakfast John tells me that Perranporth hostel had been used during the Second World War, possibly as a coast guard station, although he thinks there had been some connection with submarines. If I go and risk life and limb I can still see, if I lean far enough over the cliff, some of the structure that was left. 'It's still secret.' he says. 'No-one knows about it. The council ignore its existence and the M.O.D. have forgotten it. We're not supposed to know about its war time history'. As one can hardly miss a very prominent large white building at the edge of the cliff I'm sure that somebody knows something about it. Another one of history's hidden little gems.

It's infuriating having to delay leaving until nearly 11am for the St. Ives bus and make a detour via Land's End, but visit this I must to 'turn the corner' properly.

I take the time to book my accommodation, and having a choice of a hostel in Beer or B & B in Lyme Regis I plump for extravagance and comfort and book a B & B.

St. Ives, when I reach it, is bathed in sunshine. Now I know why artists come here, the light is so clear and bright. It's amazing. The light reflects off everything and sparkles on roof tops, the sand, the sea, even peoples faces. The roofs have acquired yellow ochre patches like drops of mustard; probably from the salt in the air or lichen and make a good contrast against the blue of sea and sky. The streets are as complicated as a jig-saw as they climb layer upon layer from the harbour where speed boats buzzing like bees zip across the water.

I have ample time to purchase tickets as far as Penzance, take a brief walk through the steep streets where I promise myself a chicken lunch in the hopes that it will be lighter on the stomach than fish and chips which, by the smell is tantalising in the extreme. On the way I have a shock when I catch sight of myself in a window. Just how long have a looked as if I have a chrysanthemum growing out of my head!? Now I know why the young female travellers take all the necessities of life on their shoulders. They carry a full hairdressing salon in their rucksacks! It will take more than a bottle of conditioner to make any sense of my top knot. Following my chicken and salad lunch I make my way back to the Malakoff for my connection for Land's End.

The journey takes me back to the bracken and the bright blue sea; patchwork fields and flowers. Twenty minutes into the run I notice an ominous smell of rubber and hear a crackling sound. I veer from cracked fan belt to total disintegration of the engine which will surely happen miles from anywhere. I am still a worrier, even after three + weeks of relative stress free solo travelling. As no-one else has sensed anything I am somewhat relieved as we motor on.

Relaxing slightly I spy some stone chimneys embedded in the ground with no evidence of buildings in the vicinity. I can't make up my mind whether these are remnants of disused tin or slate mines; when I do see remains of building plus chimney I am no wiser. It is so frustrating not to know. A thought just occurred, it would it be instructive to have a booklet of past activities, history and scenery issued with every bus journey. A sort of I SPY selection, very much like my mainstay of enjoyment when travelling by train as a child. Mulling over this lapse I am aroused by much honking of horns. There is a coach full of holiday makers closely followed by a trail of cars facing us. Although our driver sits, with a cheerfully unholy grin on his face, he is forced to back up a good fifty or so yards until the coach and its attendant comet's tail of cars has passed with the coaches other passengers making faces at us through their windows.

I wasn't expecting to change buses again: my time table didn't make a mention of it, so I was surprised when everybody was dropped off in St. Just. There is a small collection of houses and a few shops and not much else; although at first inspection it did have a rural charm about it.

A short journey later and we are at Land's End in the sunshine. Having been told that it will be as barren as John O'Groats I am overwhelmed by the hype. The number of eateries with beef burger stands, the fish and chip café's and souvenir shops in such a compact area astounds me. There is an official photographer offering a photo opportunity for those who wish to stand next to the mileage post showing the distance to London, Cape Town and New York. He is charging a fiver. Not surprisingly he is not doing a lot of trade. The contrast between here and what little I saw of John O'Groats in the rain is enormous. Probably there would have been several dozen people standing at a similar post in Scotland for the same reason in high summer. I manage not only to take a photo of the mileage post but of the first or last house (which ever way you want to look at it) in the distance. I have been sending little gifts back home, but there is a family that welcomes any post cards I send; so in a moment of madness I purchase a small transparent plastic lighthouse filled with 'sands of Cornwall'. Although it is totally useless it will be easy to pack and won't be heavy either. I'm sure they will be thrilled to death!!

As there are buses leaving here for all destinations, the drivers are driven to distraction answering questions about when and where to change. Either the bus time tables are in code or people expect a half hourly service to all points of the compass. I take pity on my driver and we take it in turns to call out 'Change at St. Just!'

With all the coming and goings I am surprised to be on the right bus for Penzance where, once again, I have a long uphill walk (all this exercise must be doing me some good) to the hostel. The hostel is warm, comfortable and welcoming. In fact it has more of a feel of a country hotel about it. Enquires made are forthcoming that it was indeed a Georgian manor which has spectacular views.

There is a large menu board showing all the different pizzas that they produce here. One of the other hostellers says that this particular hostel has the best pizzas that she has tasted, in fact the Y.H.A. handbook mentions their pizzas as a 'selling' point. The word must have got around as there is a queue at the counter. My bedroom which has just three beds, is spacious but with a distinct lack of hanging facilities. After I have unpacked, one of my room mates tells me that the showers and toilets are far enough away to warrant taking sandwiches and a hot flask. At least when I do find them the shower has directions that I can understand without leaving my glasses on to read the instructions.

The girl opposite me in our room has some interesting tales to tell about other hostels she has stayed in and we spend a pleasant half hour comparing notes before putting out our lights. Our other room mate joins us with an armful of maps and guide books just as we settle down. She says that she will be walking from St. Ives to Land's End tomorrow while she consults her guide book, borrowed

from the warden. This has been well used in the past, as it has annotations in all the areas in which she is to be walking. She proceeds to read them out to us to re-assure us that she knows what she is doing. ‘This is a steep bit, watch for steep drops’ ‘Mind the scree’ Watch out for landslip’ ‘Mind the bull.’ and other helpful hints about safe walking. She then proceeds to re-arranging her rucksack and maps in a most organised way. We have the distinct impression that she is doing it for our benefit. When she promises us that she won’t wake us up in the morning as she has to be away by 7am we nod and thank her for her consideration.

The room is unbearably hot and the bunks creak when everybody turns over. When one of us does it the others follow suit.

DAY 25. FRIDAY 18TH JULY

PLYMOUTH VIA HELSTON, TRURO AND ST. AUSTELL

As we suspected, our intrepid walker is still abed when we go down to breakfast at eight. We can't bear to wake her as she is sleeping so well.

I have a most enlivened breakfast table, sharing with Jean, a South African now a declared Aussie?, Kristen, an American girl, over here on a scholarship studying English classics; and a gentleman from the Northern Territories of Australia; none of whom are travelling together. The topics under discussion range from air travel, which we all agree on, mothers-in-law, of which we have different opinions and Shakespeare. It is nice that my start tomorrow isn't until late morning so I can spend a quiet hour writing up my notes and catching up on yet another book. We split up at the bus station where I set off for Helston, the home of the annual festival of the famous 'Flora or Furry Dance' and Truro.

I can at last switch to summer shoes which I haven't been able to wear since I got caught in the rain, although this makes me feel more like a tourist and not an intrepid traveller! It will be a pleasant experience to have time to visit Truro Cathedral which has the most beautiful Italian marble inlaid floor. What a pity that I cannot climb to the heights to photograph it. Inside on display are twelve oil on canvas pictures depicting verses from Revelations; painted by a lady who must have had a wonderful imagination. These are very powerful and in some ways surrealistic and awesome.

My bus now takes me to St. Austell where I have to change my mode of transport once again for a train to Plymouth. Whilst waiting on the platform I discover to my amazement that I have only ten days left. Where has it all gone? I have been so taken up with travel and 'sightseeing' from the comfort of bus and train, meeting new people and listening to conversations that I have been unaware of the passage of time.

There is a party of Brownies on the train along with Kristen who is amusing them with tales of America. Kristen and I alight together and find that we are both staying in the hostel. Enquiring from a local the exact location of the hostel we discover that it is miles away. Kirsten takes control and says firmly that we must take a taxi. This is a novelty. As least it will be fare sharing.

We choose our dinner selection and book breakfast as well. Again we have a super choice of food. I opt for a packed lunch for the following day as the selection is as varied as the rest of the food. I feel that I am 'splashing the cash' when Kristen considers that a bottle of wine would go down well with the evening meal and we duly go in search of a shop that will supply us. I am rather pleased to have company for once – even if it also come with her non-stop exclaiming about 'Our Will' Kristen knows 'Our Will' by reputation, by his manner, his speech, his dress, marriage and house. She just loves 'Our Will'. It is some time before I cotton on that 'Our Will' is in fact William Shakespeare. We are both somewhat light headed at the end of the meal when Kristen continues non-stop about directional qualities of Shakesperian films past and present, never mind stage productions and school interpretations. On the whole I am glad that I have had a glass or two of the red stuff as an evening with Kristen's Shakespeare is really quite enough for anybody.

There is a school group of boys staying for a night or two. Having had experience of boys en masse in hostels, I am more than pleased when then leader ensures us that all the boys should be quiet if not asleep before midnight! We have his permission to eject any that stray into our room by mistake!!

Kristen and I take a turn round the garden and once again I look at the façade and conclude that it really does look like a cinema. Inside is a large hall or foyer which has sweeping staircases with rooms off the balcony. This space has the effect of echoing like a sound box if anyone so much as sneezes. The building was owned by a banker (not a bank manager) and his household must have walked on tip toe and conversed in sign language as the whole lot of them would have been stone deaf within a month.

The young hordes arrive back from where they have been letting off steam; around ten o'clock; and drive us mad by running up and down the corridor; banging doors like drums and screeching. Kristen; never one to hold back, descends to reception and demands that something is done to quieten things down a bit. The warden has a stern word with the leader, who in turn has a stern word with the horde. Quiet descends.

DAY 26 & 27. SATURDAY 19TH & SUNDAY 20TH JULY
LYME REGIS VIA KINGSWEAR, TORQUAY, EXTER AND SIDMOUTH

The hordes got me out of bed EARLIER than necessary; they also beat both Kristen and I to the shower. Unfortunately they couldn't read and picked the girls' showers instead. Kristen let them know about their mistake in no uncertain terms. Breakfast is not a happy hour. The hordes sound as if high volume noise is all they know. Kristen keeps me company at the breakfast table. She is in full form this morning the late night having revived her. I just wish that she didn't have a habit for quoting chunks of Shakespeare at me. I had King Lear with the fruit juice; Macbeth came in with the scrambled eggs and Richard the Third arrived with the coffee. She just couldn't get away from the tragedies! If only she could have mentioned Pease Blossom and Cobweb or even Titania from 'A Midsummer Night's Dream'. I am thankful that she and I will go our separate ways before she too can become a tragedy. She is planning to take the ten past nine bus with me to Plymouth and I pay a last visit to the loo with one of the horde in close attendance. Not only can these boys not read, but this one can't even distinguish the picture of a skirted person on the wash room door.

The bus is overdue and I am beginning to panic along with other back-packers. This delay could throw everything out and I could end up with pandemonium at Sidmouth when trying to catch the last bus of the day. We are contemplating a taxi to the station and a return to the hostel to phone. Kristen really does like to organise! In amongst all the fuss and bother a local comes and informs us that we haven't missed the bus at all, it doesn't arrive until 9.40. However the taxi has been booked and three of us share the expense of a taxi to the bus station which by chance deposits me behind the very bus that I am to catch for Dartmouth for the ferry to Kingswear. The driver actually apologises if he has held me up but he had a' call of nature'. I am only too glad that nature called as I am bang on time again.

I too have a call of nature before I catch the ferry after which I only have short walk before I am seated on the top deck of an open-topped bus for Torquay.

There comes another heart-stopping bus ride through the lanes from Torquay to Exeter which seem to be only just wide enough for a hay cart and I reach the bus station within two hours. I would dearly love a coffee or a cuppa however I find all the cafés closed and the bus station is not the most comfortable place to sit as the draught is ferocious. It is becoming a fractious day and I still haven't recovered from Kristen and the hordes.

Now I am suffering another boisterous horde of teenagers or young twenty some things on the back seat which I have to endure with fortitude. I can't wait to stretch my legs at the Sidmouth triangle, which provides a very pleasant interlude before taking my final bus of the day to Lyme Regis.

A ten minutes walk from Lyme Regis Square brings me within sight of the sea. The guest house is extremely comfortable and my hostess suggests that if I can wait until her other guests have gone into the dining room for their evening meal I can have the bathroom totally undisturbed and soak as long as I like. She has even put out some bath essence for me to try. How wonderful it is to do just that; I even take a book with me and luxuriate for a full half hour. Fully refreshed I go so far as to change my T. shirt before going in search of a meal on the main street within hearing distance if not seeing distance of the sea. A light stroll to watch the tide roll in and I am back catching up on news from home; an hour's T.V. and finally a good eight hours sleep; which in itself is a luxury.

An even greater luxury is the fact that I am here for another night thanks due to the careful planning of my husband. Mind you he had written in that I might like a seven mile hike from Beer if I should care for it!

What a joy to have the time to be able to absorb the town's history, to walk the streets and view interesting places and take a walk along the river path into town to the Dinosaur Museum just on opening time. Collected and run by a palaeontologist it is a fascinating insight into local pre-history with the artefacts and information, much of which is wittily written – this is a museum where I spend over an hour increasing my knowledge of dinosaurs.

In a town like this which is full of quaint buildings there is a lot to discover. I come across the 'Gin Shop' which was formerly a store for ball and powder for

the cannon which defended the Cobb. There was a hoist high on the wall above the stone to lift both powder and shot. Just twenty yards further along is The Whispering Gallery; much like St. Paul's where there is a curved wall where whispers can be heard some way off. Some children had a whale of a time with this – if only they could have been trained to whisper; not shout! Then I came across 'Granny's Teeth'; a set of perilous steps further round the Cobb, it is said that these are mentioned in Jane Austin's novel 'Persuasion'.

I had heard that sailors were particularly superstitious, but I had never heard that they had course to worry about rabbits! A mere mention of rabbits when anyone is putting to sea might cause a catastrophe. Of course when one thinks of the Portland stone quarries and that rabbits can burrow in the cliff face one can imagine rock falls. Camera in hand I take snaps of various buildings including the 'Old Lock-Up' which has a fairy tale look about it.

Although the weather is overcast I am loath to stay indoors and walk down the sands to the Cobb and check the boats for hire. I am accosted by a hirer of boats who cons me into believing that the boat leaving shortly is for a gentle tour to view nature from the sea and was of a substantial size. It was not! I paid my money and took my ticket. I am firmly on board before I realise that it is in fact a mackerel fishing trip. I don't relish being this close to the water; not being a good swimmer I have distinct dislike of water in general. In fact I don't even take it in whisky; however there I am sitting with a fixed grin and with a family of Mum and Dad and their two small children, who are there to fish for their supper. I have a feeling that my landlady would not approve of my delivering fresh fish to her kitchen without prior warning. All goes swimmingly, until 20 or so yards out there is a slight swell. Well that's what the captain called it. It felt more like the big dipper crossed with being tossed in a blanket. I grip the rail and jam my foot against the engine cover and SMILE. I am still smiling as we rock and roll into the 'slight swell' as I become more confident in keeping my balance and start to relax I find that I am quite enjoying it and even go so far as to congratulate the boys on their fishing skills as they haul in their catch. I ask Mum to take my photo to prove to Mike that I actually sat on a very small boat and find that I have recovered my sense of fun and even that I am enjoying myself. Who would have thought it?

I am certainly in need of sustenance and I lunch off a Dorset 'pastie' and a pot of tea before I walk back to town. Visits to several shops later including an antique shop where I discus the beauty of an Edwardian belt with the proprietor. Unfortunately it is outside my price range, which is disappointing for both of us.

In my travels I had come across the odd local artists who paint so well that I can tell what it is going to be when finished. Now I have come across the most unusual of all. 'NOMAD' a psychic artist. He tell me about his paintings and how they come from 'Heaven' much like automatic writing. Although he sounds very convincing and tried his hardest to sell me one, I say that it is with regret that my rucksack wouldn't be able to hold any as most of them are on the large size. I can only hope that 'Heaven' will provide the buyers as well as giving him the inspiration to paint. Failing selling me a painting he suggests that I might like to have my psyche explored or my hand read? Not knowing just what psychic readings entail, whether it would be painful or indeed if my innermost mind would be exposed or even whether I might send off electric sparks I have to refuse his kind offer as I feel that there is rain in the wind and say that I have a good walk back to my B& B. As I walk away I also wonder what the reaction would have been if I had posted one of his pictures home?

It has been a busy morning and I relax over lunch in 'The Galley in the Alley', before trying to dodge the rain before joining my hostess for afternoon tea.

DAY 28. MONDAY 21ST JULY

PORTSMOUTH, WEYMOUTH, POOLE, BOURNEMOUTH AND SOUTHAMPTON FOR COSHAM

I filled up with breakfast, as looking at the time table my day is going to be made up of non-stop travel. I am more than pleased that my time in Lyme has been so pleasant and virtually rain free as today looks like the good English summer has caught up with me

By the time we have reached Weymouth the sun is out again and glistening on the sea. I am all fresh and content with life – and then – I have my first major blip since I left Scotland. The bus going to Poole does not exist. Another doesn't go the way I want it to and a yet another stops half way there. Time for action! There is really no need for me to change in Poole as I can go straight to Bournemouth so I head for the Express office where I book a ticket, making sure that my further connection will be on the time table. I also have qualms about finding buses in London for Ipswich. I get worried in big cities and will surely lose myself in the busy streets even if the bus station is located directly across from my connection. A possibility is that I can book an express from London to Ipswich from Weymouth. I make tentative enquiries. Wonderful news; there is no problem about booking a seat. The relief is awesome, it would have been a great source of worry when I arrived in London.

I have time for lunch and a pause sitting on the breakwater watching a young mother trying to persuade her little daughter to jump down all of three feet; which to her must feel like the top of Blackpool Tower. We end up by holding a hand each as she jumps down. She is so pleased with herself afterwards and can't wait to do it again – and again.

Later I come up against yet another obstacle. Bournemouth Square is nowhere near Bournemouth Triangle; this leaves me with no option but to resort to an EXPRESS once again for Southampton. After the easy connections and smooth transport I have encountered n the north this is not the experience I expected in the supposedly better organised south for its transport systems. Problems become even more complicated when I arrive in Southampton. There seems to be total chaos in the city centre. Is it a reconstruction of the entire place? There are cranes, diversions and major road works. I am badly misdirected and arrive hot, tired and fed up at the railway station. The only piece of luck, if one can call it that, is the fact that I have only half an hour to wait for the train to Cosham.

Outside Cosham railway station I endeavour to ask assistance from a couple of German visitors, who struggle with the word 'map' in their vocabulary. Realising that a cartographer is a maker of maps I cudgel my brain and come up with the word 'karte'. At least my brain is working if not the rest of me. One of them says excitedly 'Ein Karte ! We have that Ja!.' and produces a 'mini-map. Together we try to make sense of their 'mini-map' As neither of us knows exactly where we are even when turning the paper upside down I have little option but to set off hopefully in the right direction and arrive at the hostel in a state that can only be regarded as pathetic. What makes matters worse is that I have missed the evening meal. The warden and his wife are NOT helpful nor can they give me any advice as to where I may get a meal in a pub or restaurant. I can hear voices from what I take to be a dining room. Somebody is eating at any rate. These are two of the most taciturn wardens I have met who run a hostel. They glare at us, say little or 'yes' or 'no' when asked a question. They are NOT your average welcome greeting party. They tell us that they are retiring at the end of the season. – We consider that it's not before time – Then they take our breaths away by stating that they are taking up a B & B on the south coast.

My bed made after a restorative shower I go in search of food. I meet a most helpful young man with long hair and a sheepskin jacket who, figuratively takes me by the hand and leads me in the direction of a pub. Here I have a super steak washed down by a glass of beer. Now I feel more inclined on my return to take a good look at the hostel which has the frontage of a proper country manor; a spacious hall and sweeping staircase to one side with several rooms off the hall, all of which smell musty and damp. Information gathered on a small brochure is that Wymering Manor goes as far back as Edward the Confessor in 1042. I can see why it is now a Grade II listed building. There had also been talk of ghosts; Sir Roderick or Reckless Roddy who was lying headless on the steps outside. There was also mention of a horse who may have been headless, galloping down the lane its hooves sparking on the cobbles. There was also a tale of a choir of nuns singing in the hall. If there was I never felt so much as a whisper, nor any change in temperature. If there are any ghosts they were welcome to play and sing to their hearts content. I will not disturb them if they leave me alone. I was still feeling depressed, fraught and very, very tired.

The tone of my voice when I ring home to check for the umpteenth time for directions on tomorrow's time table makes Mike concerned. I am at my lowest ebb and I request that if he knows of a helicopter coming my way he will allow it to collect me and bring me home. We blow kisses down the phone.

After that I had sufficient presence of mind to ask the warden to book my food and accommodation for the next two hostels before collapsing on my bed.

DAY 29. TUESDAY 22ND JULY
DOVER VIA HAVANT AND BRIGHTON

I have totally forgotten the information gathered yesterday, and I have to ring Mike at 7.30am. This does not help at all when I discover that the train from Cosham to Havant does not run at all – if it ever did – it must have been a figment of the imagination all along. There are however buses which run every 10 or 15 minutes. Missing my bus by seconds does not improve my day in the least. My thoughts calm down somewhat when the next bus takes me nicely to Havant and happily the stop for my next bus is directly behind me. (with just a ten minute wait). I am still trying to come to terms with the past fraught and tiring 24 hours and I can't really take in much of the surrounding towns and scenery. I have a faint recollection that we went through Fishbourne; It is a pity that I couldn't take in any information or notice signs to anywhere historic as this is another town that would hold my interest because of its Roman Palace. One can view Roman mosaics and forts in many areas of Britain, but how I would have loved to visit a Palace! Perhaps someone would have re-done the formal gardens. Would there have been any remains of a fountain? This part of England must have had so many Roman remains; both large and small.

We enter Chichester yet another stronghold. They got everywhere, these Romans, laying out street plans and building villas. But there is more to Chichester than Roman Britain with its elegant Georgian town houses (my favourite design) which also will have no doubt, a well stocked museum somewhere in the city. Although we have strayed from the coast, the towns that we have passed through have tickled my imagination.

The weather is breaking up and I have difficulty in spotting any boats on the sea or in the harbour in Littlehampton. We are back with a seaside view as the cloud builds and disperses. Patches of blue with cream streaks tinge the horizon allowing me to relax once more as we approach Worthing. Whenever I get a glimpse of an interesting row of buildings the bus veers off down streets of shops. It is frustrating to think of all this architecture being lost to me. More to the point I am now reverting back to the original time table as trains and helicopters are forgotten. We arrive in Bournemouth 15 minutes late which means I now have a choice: food or toilet, both in opposite directions. I think that my time table means that I will be on the bus for several hours I rush like an express train through Marks and Spencers for the loo. I certainly couldn't go for 5 hours without a comfort stop but I can manage without food; I hope.

I find that I have not quite recovered from my stay at Wymering Manor and I keep dropping off to sleep and missing bits. The views are getting disjointed and sometimes I feel that we have passed the same place twice or that the bus has gone astray completely. I now have a stiff neck and try reading, if only to keep me awake so that I know when to alight.

The long and rather tedious journey over I find to my delight that I have only a 10 – 15 minute walk to Dover hostel – my spirits could do with a lift.

Well, this is surprising: here I am only a mile from one of the busiest terminal ports in the world and I come across a Georgian building which has a smart portico and neat, square windows. This is the Youth Hostel and on entering I find that it is as humid as a Swedish sauna. Can it really be as hot as this? People are actually glowing, the heat haze is misting my glasses and I can't take in the effusive welcome in reception. Somebody points me in the direction of the dining room, the lounge, even where I can order Euro's or buy ferry tickets; should I require them. I am given my bedding which I am pleased to have a sheet and not sleep-bags. I measured the last sleep-bag from the pillow case section, and if it measured 5 feet I'll eat that next duvet I come across. I am told where I am to sleep. The hostel is on three floors and I think I am put on the middle floor facing the front. Due to poor lighting and my steamed up glasses I cannot see much in the gloom.

I know that I have a bed and I am sharing a room with at least two others, although like many hostellers, their bags take up more space than they do. The receptionist was right everyone is very friendly in the dining room, although it is a struggle to understand the various languages and dialects that zip across the table. I retire for the night but I cannot in all honesty say that I, nor any of the others sharing my room, got much sleep. The heat was a tropical high. What the hostel used for heating was anyone's guess. Perhaps they had their own personal coal mine or had found oil beneath the cellars? We tried opening the window – This was a grave mistake – As there seemed to be a collection of motor cyclists practising for the T.T. who went screaming down the road. We suffered. I had to recourse to visit the toilet during the night and creeping down the stair well I bumped into two girls coming in from the Continent and three other girls leaving. They must have had an early start if they were packing their things around two in the morning.

A thought here about toilets, both in particular and in general. Most public toilets situated in town and cities can very in size and facilities. Some have doors that will only open with arms that have the strength of ten men and some that you would need an army to close. There are those that have too many protuberances; ie waste bin, nappy or sanitary receptacle, a toilet roll holder and, in some, spare toilet rolls. Sitting down one has to be double joined at the very least whilst hugging whatever bags you came in with. There are those, of course that have run out of paper and those that have a mat of it. Not forgetting those whose doors do not lock. I had come across some where I had to balance rucksack and holdall on my knee as the floor was awash. Occasionally I encountered the well maintained sparklingly clean toilets with wash basins, soap and hand dryer. But in the main I had to get used to manoeuvring my way in and out without causing damage to myself. Now, in the Dover hostel, I came across cubicles which gave all the instructions in more than one language. The use of the toilet: the soap dispenser; the use and disposal of used toilet paper and where no doubt to put the baby! It is very strange what one encounters on one's travels, even in the loo.

On The Way Up

DAY 30. WEDNESDAY 23RD JULY
STRATFORD ST. ANDREW & BLAXHALL VIA LONDON AND IPSWICH

A car alarm frightens the life out of the whole room at 3.30 and I do the whole stairwell walk over again, meeting more foreigners en route for their gap year in Britain.

By the time my colleagues and I have woken sufficiently in time for breakfast we all look as if we had been at an all night party which we have not enjoyed very much.

Breakfast conversation runs to the exciting times that some will have when they reach Belgium, France, Italy and further afield. My time is slowly coming to an end but I mange to entertain my fellow eaters with one to two reminiscences of my travel before we all leave for different modes of transport.

The receptionist tells me my bus leaves from Breeds Place not Pencester road. Further information is confusing as to exactly where this is and I waste valuable time in looking it up in an A to Z book in reception.

The bus is gently steaming with passengers drying out their damp clothing, and I have to share my seat with a young man who, like me has a rucksack plus assorted packages. Together we manage to take up a lot of floor space between our feet, apologising as we do so. He, like me, is getting off in London and will be looking for relatives who are putting him up for the night before he starts his 'gap year' in Holland. I notice that he too must have had a sleepless night as within half an hour he is dozing while I manage to do the same. Thankfully we will both be getting off at the terminus or one of us could end up anywhere.

My coach disgorges us at a minor offshoot of Victoria Coach Station where we, along with the world and his wife, find that it is raining cats and dogs. I am amused by the difference between the nationalities by the way they view the weather. The Japanese hustle together and search for hoods and umbrella's before venturing outside chattering and laughing. Americans, by and large puff out their cheeks and link arms and walk carefully and steadily through the downpour. They must think that the English rain might hurt by the way they scowl at the clouds. Germans and Northern Europeans charge through the rain as if it didn't exist. We British, well we just shrug our shoulders having seen a lot of it we are used to the wet weather but we still cower and curl our shoulders as if it frightens us.

Not having been in London since 1960 this is quite an experience; my eyes are everywhere and I find that I have difficulty in jotting down my view of the townscape before we turn corners and a new set of buildings catches my eye. One thing that did catch my eye was a large shopping centre at Eccleston Square which resembled enormous 'glass containers' stacked on top of one another. Was this an economy measure? Had the constructors run out of building materials? Did the architect really think that he or she wanted it to stand out amongst the neat classical buildings surrounding it? Whatever the reason it certainly stands out and catches not only the eye but the sunshine. Amazing!

The creamy stone buildings become London very well; a constant sense of stateliness and prosperity. From my vantage point I can see the care and attention to detail of the stonemason's art. From the corbels to fluted columns, the window embrasures and roof lines to chimney pots. What artisan could design such work on a computer? Would they bother to spend the time? Would anyone nowadays appreciate their efforts? I feel lucky that I can glimpse these stone carvings at eye level when we pause for the lights or are in a traffic queue.

We have a mini tour of London ahead of us. The Houses of Parliament; Lambeth Bridge; Horse Guards Parade with the immobile men on their equally immobile mounts. We also pass Cleopatra's Needle and the Sphinx. The City of London School and the rear end of the Mermaid Theatre. We even manage a peek of 'Sir John Lyon House. The words 'the very centre of the tea trade' across the frontage of a building. Who was Sir John Lyon? Was he John Lyon, merchant of Preston, founder of Harrow School and other charities for young people. Did Good Queen Bess knight him for his good works? We pass this building too quickly for me to gather any further information.

Even if I had a street map and had the time to look at the street names as we pass I would lose my way here; we are passing places that I had only ever heard about or read in novels. Now we are at College Street with its mini colourful garden and fountain where the newest generation are as attracted to the water as were their parents. I can hear laughter mixed in with the drizzle; a musical sound as the youngsters enjoy the water. Upper and Lower Thames Street where cubism has gone mad: stone, marble and glass break forth into the latest construction ideas. Where does this influence come from? The art students' imagination seem to bypass inspiration from history or any past architects. Do we have to sacrifice beauty for modernism I wonder? Or am I, getting to the stage of distrusting the 'new idea'? After all each generation of artistic thought has had its own ideas of what should or could be built and what shape it could be. Art Deco was a thought too far for some, as was the 1950's with colour and design. Someday, someone will come up with a compromise and someone else will disagree with it as an eyesore.

I thought however that All Hallows by the Tower could have been improved with a good wash and brush up. The Tower of London, which does not look as foreboding as pictures and history will have us believe surrounded as it is, with the grandiose temples of commerce blends in rather well. It's hard to think of the many people who lost their heads there.

Now we approach an area where all the nations meet like tides of the sea! We are slowly passing an international street market, where the traditionalists wear the attire of their native country. Colourful shirts, saris, caftans and turbans, their bright and vibrant clothes really lift the day. All are hugger-mugger behind their stalls with boxes of goods and trays of food. Some are gesticulating to passers by encouraging them to taste, or examine their produce, each stall holder looking happy and smiling. We could be anywhere where it is hot and sunny. Their stands are full of the knick-knacks and other goods which I can't quite make out, possibly fruit or vegetables. One or two are on mobile phones; are they perhaps negotiating the best price of yams, watermelons, paw-paw or just making a date for that night? Every street market should have at least two or three West African or Jamaican stalls set out with colour and vibrancy. Suddenly we break free of the past and into a modern mish mash of flats; business offices and car-parks. What a contrast!

Without warning we are at Stratford which has a beautiful bus station with fan vaulting, looking like lotus flowers, holds up the interior of the roof as it stretches over the people waiting for the buses. Arched tendrils meet and trail down to the columns. Now here is what I call beauty in a forgotten place. How many passengers would look up at the graceful structure above their heads? Ah well!

A further ten minutes of travel and we are out of the City of London. This unintentional 'tour' through London means that we arrive in Ipswich bus station over thirty minutes late and I have less than a quarter of a hour to locate my bus for Stratford St. Andrew and Blaxhall Youth Hostel.

There are few buses left in the bus station at this time of day, none of which indicate that they are heading for Stratford St. Andrew. The station office is closed and the only passengers are standing in groups and smile at me when I go and enquire if they can help. I am directed from one group to another, each group asking me if I require Stratford St. Mary. 'NO I DON'T, THANK YOU'. I have never heard of Stratford St. Mary and this is time wasting and frustrating to say the least. No-one had ever heard of a youth hostel in any case. Each person I ask has a smiling face and I have the feeling that I am in a science fiction movie or a parallel universe where everyone was programmed to say the same thing. Or even be transported to another planet. Hunting out a bus mechanic who has his arm in an engine I ask him for help. None is forthcoming. Now I ring the hostel and they suggest I get the Saxmundham bus,' But, of course' the warden said. 'There will be a five mile walk to the hostel and you will miss the evening meal.'

I can hear in the background, the warden rustle paper. Then he said. 'There is an alternative, you could wait at the bus station and catch a later bus and arrive after 9.pm' I thank him for the information and switch off my phone while I work something out. I refuse to be beaten there must be another way round this conundrum. This has turned into another BLIP in the system.

The Saxmundham bus is idling its engines and the driver is having a cigarette. How well does he know Saxmundham? He knows the area very well he says and is sure that there is a certainty of accommodation in the town. Checking my time table I discover that I have to change buses in Saxmundham tomorrow missing out Blaxhall and Tunstall en route. Tunstall can do without me for once as I dump my rucksack on the bus and ring to cancel my night at the hostel.

We trundle through the pretty country lanes where, before long, I see a road sign that points to Stratford St. Andrew and a finger post points to Blaxhall just 2 miles down the lane. Words fail me! My driver kindly drops me off outside a hotel and I briefly explain my next destination to the driver. Of course this is the one man I should have asked right at the beginning as he too is flummoxed by the ignorance of the Ipswich passengers. He goes so far as to show me where I can get the bus for Lowestoft the next morning. The hotel offering B & B has Tourist Board Status with several stars which even without checking is going to be out of my price range. There is a pub and the police station which is closed for the day and in any case would be connected by an outside telephone to Felixtow or Ipswich. Not wishing to disturb the machinations of the rural police force I re-assess the possibilities of spotting a house which might offer me a night when I see the White Hart Pub which I had passed on the way. Yes they have a room and at an acceptable price, we shake hands and the deal is done. My first thought is 'A Pint of your best, please landlord' as I put in a request before going to sit at a table in a tiny fish and chip café and take-away for a well deserved supper.

DAY 31 & 32. THURSDAY 24TH & 25TH JULY
SHERINGHAM VIA LOWESOFT, GREAT YARMOUTH AND NORWICH

Loath as I am to leave my comfortable bed where I have slept the sleep of the just I pack up my belongings and present myself in the dining room where I was expected to put away enough food to see me through a five mile hike. I have now only four days left, but with a full stomach and a light heart at the prospect of seeing the sea once again, say a grateful thank you to my host I walk the short distance to the bus. As luck would have it the bus and I arrive at the same time and once again I am on schedule and although a little sad that my journey is almost over, the next few days should give me that little lift especially as the sun is shining once again.

I have three wonderful hours to explore a little of Lowestoft where the only downside is where to start. Fishing trawlers always have a fascination for me with their yards of netted ropes, engines and other mechanical parts. The smell to a landlubber is reminiscent of not only sea and ships but adventure; although I am sure that if it were my livelihood I would get sick of it soon enough. The sandy pleasure beach near the harbour entrance even has a children's corner where I can see small children playing. I find that I have whiled away a good half hour watching happy children enjoying themselves. It brings back memories of my childhood in the sand, while the sun is bringing out all the flowers in the gardens. I manage to stroll a little way toward the cobbled streets known as 'The Scores' before heading back for my bus after a last look at the harbour, where I enjoyed a leisurely fish and chip lunch en route, which thinking about it is only the second 'seaside' meal I've had.

I will have a brief stop in Norwich which is further inland than I had wished to go. However I cannot dictate the bus route and I am so pleased that the bus company thought I might like to visit Norwich. It has one of the country's most beautiful cathedrals. It takes my breath away as it stands proudly in its grounds. The carved stone bosses alone are worth taking note of with their Biblical scenes and grotesque creatures. I just can't grasp the work that has gone into the carving or the hours spent. I can well believe that this cathedral was started between 1094-6. It would have taken the architect all that time to draw in all that he wanted. This is yet another city which I will note in my 'visit again' book. I just had time to be directed to the burial site of Nurse Edith Cavell, executed as a spy in Belgium in 1915. Her story is a sad one: spy or heroine? It all depends on your perspective and your country I suppose. I was sorry I had to bypass the 'Unique Mustard Shop' and its museum as I had heard that another shop cum café was selling the best ice creams in the city. There was no question which one I was going for! I sat and enjoyed an ice cream in a tall glass with a long spoon (I remember when knickerbocker glories were to be had for 7/6d and cones were 4d) before going and hopefully 'choosing' a bus for Sheringham.

They have a novel way with buses at Norwich bus station. Rather than buses having designated stands in an orderly fashion, which although obvious, lacks novelty appeal a driver, who presumably chooses a route that he fancies, picks the bus he prefers and stands in the middle of the bus station calling for passengers to go wherever he has selected. (Crumbs, imagine 'All aboard for sunny Clacton) I am not sure though, they might have to toss for it. On reflection there must be a logical reason for the apparent look of disorganisation. The single decker I boarded was the prettiest, cleanest bus I had seen or been on. A sweet shade of pale turquoise and light purple, I felt that I had risen to great heights travelling on that bus.

We are slowly making our way back to the coast once again and stop briefly in Cromer before heading north to Sheringham. The bus driver sets me down at a stop near the hostel. 'To save your legs m'dear' he said kindly saving me a long walk from the town centre.

I sign in after the warden, who is going into town, offers to walk with me and show me the Tourist Office as I am to have two nights here and there will be things to do and things to see. She has a wealth of knowledge about Sheringham and the hostel.

'It was built in the 1890's as a Roman Catholic school, the building containing not just the school but the chapel with a beautiful stained glass window' she says. 'No one knows quite what took place between that time and the early 1940's. I couldn't find any information about its history which is a pity because I'm sure that it was still in use as either as a school or a place of worship' she continued 'When the building was re-opened it was as a home for war time single mothers who were looked after by nuns. New mums would come to give birth and after they had reached one month old the babies would be put up for adoption. To help pay for their stay the mothers would help the incomers for 6 months. The mother's and babies home was still in action until 1975 when there were only 3 babies left being cared for by 8 nuns. The mothers must have been looked after very well as some returned to visit the nuns and thank them for their care'.

What a pleasant place it must have been and what a welcome the nuns must have given the mothers to be.

The warden carries on. 'The building was then put up for auction and fierce competition was expected, but the only ones to attend for the bidding were Y.H.A. officials. The offer put in was £42,000 and was this was finally excepted. A further £40,000 was needed before it was turned into a hostel and field study centre'.

The warden says that I must take a look through the door of the church and see the window which is still in place. As we part company she asks where my next hostel is. When I say that it is in Hunstanton, she smiles and says that the wardens there will entertain me and be sure to ask them about the kitchen ceiling.

The Tourist Information Office has a wealth of information about Sheringham which has thrived on the fishing industry especially lobsters, crabs and whelks.

They also have brochures on what is happening this weekend and I find that I can by chance have two concerts and I can buy tickets for both at the desk. One is for the 'Tuesday Singers' and the other is for the 'Sheringham Shanty Men' on consecutive nights. In the town there are of course plenty of shops including a craft centre which has some lovely wood carvings in Hibiscus wood, of a 'loving couple' in different sizes and facing each other. Very little detail but very tactile. The purchase of this beautiful thing is going to overstretch my budget and will be a nuisance to carry. However it is so lovely and I think of Mike and I together and I push all guilt to one side and splash out the £25 and I hope that he will appreciate my thought and love.

I ask a passer by about the directions to St. Peter's Road and St. Peter's Church where the concert tonight is featuring the 'Tuesday Singers' who are going to do 'Songs from the Shows' This local inhabitant not only has me confused but herself as well as she can't make up her mind which is right or left. I thank her for her time and leave her still trying to work it out on her fingers. Having a brain wave I enquire at a house agents where I am given clear directions.

On returning to the hostel I remember to look through the chapel door at the stained glass window which is truly beautiful. I am impressed that it is still there and being preserved. So many have gone to other places or been taken apart.

The dining room is obviously very popular as there is a considerable queue. I place my order and as I am waiting I notice that they have one of my favourite desserts. Pineapple topped with meringue and cream on a sponge base if I have room for it as my dinner plate is well filled. I can't resist temptation and go to put in a request for pudding which is done especially to order. My head is in a book as a chef, a rather a large lady brings it to me. I say a polite 'Thank you' to which she replies, leaning close and winking a eye. 'Anything for YOU ducks. as she lays it in front of me. This leaves me wondering whether my request or my appearance is causing some emotion!

I get to St. Peter's Church in good time which is just as well as the Tuesday Singers seem to be very popular. Named The Tuesday Singers because the ladies can only meet up for their rehearsal on Tuesdays. All very logical. I am still the humming tunes as I prepare for bed.

Showers and I don't get on very well. The instructions can usually be read only when reading them with my glasses on which I then forget to take off until my face is covered in soap suds. Either the water is too hot or it cannot be turned up or down or the shower head is all twisted out of shape. No, duvets and showers are to be avoided if at all possible. The shower this morning is working on a strict economy measure as it spurts out water for 7 seconds before the button has to be pushed again. This is the only flaw that I can find in the hostel, as all together it is a wonderful place and I only wish that I could stay longer.

I take in yet another film for

processing and, feeling the need for exercise and the weather being glorious, I walk the entire length of the prom and back and then, in a mad spurt, follow the coastal path for some distance before returning, collecting my film and having lunch in town.

Sheringham at the east side is dotted with little white painted cottages with their flower filled window boxes; little alley ways and by-ways pop up when they are not expected and I have a feeling that I am trespassing on private land by going round corners and up steps. I could be in a land of charming fairy houses.

There is always the attraction of book shops and I have just come to the end of yet another book. I wonder just how many I have read this trip; how many have I sent home and how many have I donated to the hostels?

I shall welcome a sit down after my strenuous walk but after all the bus journeys, and now the good food in England I am convinced that I am putting on all the weight that I took off in Scotland.

There were over a hundred people attending that evenings' event for the Sheringham Shanty Men. Their popularity is evident by the rapturous applause at the end of their concert. Originally made up from sea faring men they are now recruited from other professions as well as fishermen. My neighbour says that they are very well known internationally and across America. It was an absolute delight to be able to catch both the 'Shanty Men' and the 'Tuesday Singers', especially as they were both 'home grown'.

DAY 33. FRIDAY 26TH JULY
HUNSTANTON

I have elected to catch a mid morning bus so that I can enjoy my last good breakfast and the pleasure of being in Sheringham. This is another place that I have added on to my 'visit again' diary. There will only be one bus journey today, for which I am very thankful. There have been some days where I have lost count of the number of buses and couldn't really keep track of just where I was in the scheme of things. Some of the towns, especially inner cities have had me confused. If it hadn't have been for my trusty time table I shouldn't have known one town from another. The countryside has lifted my spirits time and time again, the changes in floral banks and fields, the opening of buds and foliage as I travelled further south. The long distance views of hill and moorland, sea and sky. It has all been wonderful.

Chatting with the warden after breakfast she reminds me to ask at Hunstanton hostel about the ceiling episode, and I promise that I will. She amuses me by telling me stories of past wardens in other hostels that she has known and the demands of hostellers. She talks of hostels so remote that helicopters were used for food drops! The wardens that carried gas bottles on their backs for miles and hostellers who arrived out of season with out of date YHA hand books who demanded accommodation including early morning tea. I can hardly contemplate the patience and unvoiced thoughts of the hostel wardens that catered for those hardy souls who like to trek in the wilderness. Mike has stayed at such isolated hostels half a mile or so from their car parks and carried his rucksack on his back.

This bus journey is enlivened by an elderly lady passenger sitting next to me with as we swap holiday anecdotes. She is quite excited that I have travelled alone and for so long, then she tells me about her adventures. She has a lady friend with whom she goes abroad occasionally. They met at a church whist drive and started having coffee together, then a day out once a fortnight. Their friendship grew and they planned on a weekend away. Their families approved. They said it was getting her out of the house and it was good to have a friend. Then the idea took that they should go abroad for a week in the sun. Had her relatives said that they were starting up a drug ring or importing stolen goods their news couldn't have gone down any worse. Both sides got together and tried to persuade them not to go. 'We don't know what you might get up to' their relatives said. 'We were only going to Spain!' replied my acquaintance. 'Of course what they really feared was that we might pick up a toy boy each.' my companion gave a wicked grin. I asked if they did go in the end. 'You bet!' she said, 'We go twice a year and we love it.'

We now pass through small villages and hamlets, with sign posts that apparently lead nowhere in particular. One that just states BY ROAD. Is that an indication that the only access to somewhere is by road! How else would one expect to arrive at their destination? Then there is 'Old Woman's Lane' There's a puzzler for you? Who was this 'Old Woman' someone somewhere knows the answer.

Perhaps this Old Woman happened to be the local witch, white of course. Past Blakeney village with the two towers of the parish church, spotted miles before we reach it. It is said that this second tower was constructed as a lighthouse. A passenger asks me if I had noticed the tide mark on one of the houses near the quay. I hadn't but I did remember that Blakeney was overwhelmed by the floods in 1953 when there was a huge tidal surge which destroyed countless houses and caused huge destruction. Next came Weybourne and Clay next the Sea. Every town we pass through is 'Next the Sea'. Then a sign post for Great Walsingham. I'm sure that I had a momentary glimpse of a sign that says Orthodox Church of the Transgressor. I wonder if this is Greek Orthodox? If so it is a strange place to have one. Back inland again a trifle to Stiffkey, apparently the locals pronounce it 'Stewkey'. We have a delightful diversion at Holkham Hall when the bus manoeuvres through the very narrow gates and up the drive through the park to the Hall where it turns around for the return journey. Picnicers are everywhere on the grass enjoying the sunshine and I am nearly sure that I spotted a deer or two hiding behind some of the trees. Although the panorama of cropped grass and lake set off the Palladian hall, which was open to the public was glorious enough I would dearly have loved to have had some time there. I kept on seeing snapshot views of the sea as we wend our way past signs for Burnham Norton, Dunham Deepdale, Brancaster, Thornton and Holme-next-the-Sea. I am positive that I also caught sight of a sign to Creake Abbey. History must abound in this neck of the woods and I am travelling too fast to see any of it. Mike was right. A trip like this should be done at leisure and every interesting place investigated.

It is well after lunch time when I arrive in Hunstanton so I hunt out a café, hopefully with a toilet, before going down to the prom. The hostel will not open its doors until 5pm so I will have to amuse myself for a few hours at least. The promenade is very long with sadly lacking tea rooms or pleasant views. There is only a kiosk selling the usual postcards, buckets, spades and sun hats. The tide is very far out which leaves the promenading families with nothing but sand to look at. No paddling today. An elderly lady sits beside me and we discuss the lack of floral arrangements and the difference between the children of today with those of yesteryear. 'We knew what to do with sand.' she says. 'We found that not only could we make sandcastles but construct cars and boats which from distance looked almost real. What is a pity is that parents today can't be bothered to play with their children. It's very sad.' We look at the bored parents with their bored children just walking up and down the prom. Each time they pass us they look so fed up and miserable. Holidays on the beach do not have the same attraction nowadays that I had enjoyed as a child.

It is dead on five o'clock when I present myself at the hostel when suddenly a young man is standing with his arms open and he cries out 'Hello I'm Jules, this is my friend….' His friend who mutters his name in French disappears into the kitchen and sounds as if he is giving instructions in French to somebody else. I am overcome by Jules who is effusive with his welcome. Arm round my shoulder he ushers me into the hall and offers me fresh coffee as soon as I have filled in the requisite forms. Jules has taken my breath away, as I wasn't used to such a warm welcome in any of the hostels. He takes me upstairs and explains some of the rules of the 'house'. I am put in the girl's side of the two houses that make up the hostel, the boys side is on the right and has no access to the top floors.

'All I ask is that there is no noise after eleven o'clock and everything is put away in the lounge, no muddy boots in the lounge and bedding is to be put in the laundry box' he says. 'I've given you a quiet room. Coffee will be ready as soon as you come down. Oh! By the way, do you like red wine?' I nod hopefully. 'Good' he continues. 'The cook of the day; not me dear, will be opening a bottle of red wine for the dish of the day which is coq au vin. He did think of making it just with cream but would you like a glass?' 'Thank you very much that's very kind.' I assure him and tell him that I will be down shortly. As he is leaving he is insistent that I have the pudding as his friend has gone to a special effort in making it. I promise that however full I am I will have the pudding.

Dinner is somewhat delayed as the three of us – I never did discover the friend's name - sat in the little garden where we put the world to rights and went on to talk about word travel. They had moved around a lot these two, and went into raptures over the Continent in general with France in particular. Australia got a fair hearing too. We delved into the Euro, the Common Market, the Exchange rate and the cost of living. The glass of wine developed into three and finally we killed the bottle. The coq au vin was delicious as was the pudding, both brought to me by an assistant. After dinner I ask Jules about the ceiling episode as the

last warden in Sheringham has asked me to refer to it. Jules and friend take me into the kitchen and stand shoulder to shoulder in a pose that reminds me of Tweedlee and Tweedledum . Jules then explains at some length that they had put in for renovations for some months and were getting nowhere. 'It's the kitchen that needed it most.' says his friend with a strong French intonation, 'We had at last persuaded some one from head office to come and inspect it. He stood right here dear, just where we are standing.' His foot tapped the lino. 'He said that there was nothing wrong, perhaps just a new coat of paint would do. Just then the ceiling fell in and covered him with plaster. The look on his face was a picture. It took us ages and ages to brush him down dear, we just couldn't stop laughing.'

'Then we got a new ceiling and a repainting too. But we couldn't use the kitchen for weeks.' finished Jules.

They were still chuckling over this episode six months later.

I contact home and I am please to talk to Mike at some length and intrigued when he says that he will meet me in Mablethorpe and will have something he wants me to see. My begging him to tell me doesn't sway him; all will be revealed when me meet.

DAY 34. SATURDAY 27TH JULY
MABLETHORPE VIA KINGS LYNN, SPALDING AND BOSTON

A couple who joined me for breakfast had spent the weekend getting each other fit by walking themselves into the ground. The girl was more used to putting one foot in front of the other so it was her boyfriend that had to be encouraged for the last ten miles. He was suffering, he said, and was not sure that his knees would take him as far as the office desk the following morning. He looked more in need of a complete massage than bacon and eggs. We chatted so long over the coffee that I was in danger of missing my bus to King's Lynn. I gave a final wave to my friends as I hurried out of the door. I felt sorry for the man, who would remember those last ten miles for some time to come.

Jules comes to the door to wave goodbye and as I leave a thought crosses my mind that I have just met a modern version of Julian and Sandy from 'Round the Horne' or Beyond Our Ken' in the nicest way possible.

I can still see the sea on my right and a long stretch of sand leading to a notice of an RSPB viewing site with the delightful name of Ingoldsthorpe. They certainly had imagination round here, or indeed the name might have meant something in pre-medieval days. We are moving slowly inland as we go through Dersingham and over the Babingley River, past the castle or bits of it, at Castle Rising and get caught up in traffic getting in to King's Lynn. This might look as if it is inland, but in fact it is a port and has been since the Middle Ages. We stop in the centre long enough for me to admire the ornate building in the market place. King's Lynn was damp as was the air, the people, and the toilets. It seemed to be in a perpetual state of just emerging from the water. The only place that was dry was the bus enquiry office. Here I am swamped with more alternatives of travel. The more I tried to decipher the time table the more confused I became. The easy route didn't seem that easy standing in a queue with those behind champing at the bit, shuffling from one leg to the other and muttering to each other. I find that it is easier giving my final destination of the day to the girl behind the grill and letting her sort it out. There was a minor disruption as six of us boarded and we all only had notes to offer for our tickets, so the first four received a glower from the driver. I couldn't very well get off for change or I might have missed the connection. The driver repeated to each of us that we would get our change later when he had some more passengers 'offering the right change!'

An elderly gentleman sits in front of me and I ask him if he knows anything about the Dutch style building which is near by. It was built, he says, in 1683 and the statue over the doorway is of Charles II and it was once the Customs House. He is disappointed when I tell him that I am going further and will not have time to visit it, St. Margaret's Church nor the Town Hall, or even the Guildhall which was built in 1420 never mind all the other fascinating buildings in the town. Once again I have come to the conclusion that Mike was right. We would have added on several weeks of travel if not months investigating all the towns that I have passed through.

We are curving gently round the Wash but so far inland that I can't make out the sea at all. Entering Long Sutton there is a sign to the Tropical Gardens with a wild-flower meadow which I am sure will be ablaze at this time of year.

The countryside claims us once more as we head towards Boston. This is another part of the country that I am not familiar with so I will have to have my eyes peeled for the famous St. Botolph's Church, known as The Boston Stump. Craning my neck to an impossible angle I am impressed with its shape and size. This action has amused an elderly lady in the opposite seat who is a resident. We strike up a conversation about the town and her involvement with the local W.I. and speakers that she has encountered over the years. She had been lucky to have seen Joyce Grenfell on stage and can remember some of her renditions. At a literary luncheon that year she actually met Edwina Currie after her listening to her talk. 'A very amusing lady, she could talk on just about any subject and make it entertaining. Do try to catch her if you can, she is well worth listening to.'

We part company in Skegness, another seaside town that is a surprise to me. Although I am familiar with the old British Rail posters telling people to come to Skegness ('It's so Bracing') for their holidays. I had always thought that it was the invention of the local Council promoting the area. Skegness is stunning even though the weather isn't doing it justice, now being somewhat overcast, however I can tell it's 'bracing' by the number of people holding on to their coats to keep out the 'bracing' air. The houses that we pass are of a Victorian solidarity and handsome with it. The tree lined avenues are in full leaf and all it wants are ladies in crinolines and men in top hats to finish the picture. I have to change buses here for Mablethorpe and as it is way past the lunch hour my meal is of a scratch variety but I make time to take a look at the bustling sea front and promenade with its floral displays. The posters were right – come to Skegness – You won't be disappointed.

As I wait for my bus I realise that hearth and home will feel a little tame after my adventures. A world wide traveller I met in Sheringham rightly remarked that once you start travelling the bug hits you and your feet begin to itch for the open road. However I have the wonders of Mablethorpe to look forward to and seeing my husband who sounded quite excited at the prospect.

Mike is there waiting at the bus station with a great smile and open arms. I find that I have indeed missed him as much as he has missed me. He has booked us both in to a B & B which will round my adventures off nicely. There is such a lot to catch up on even though we have spoken virtually every day. First there is the matter of an evening meal when he treats me to steak and chips. I am dying to know just what it is that he has to show me. He insists however that we do a tour of the seaside resort and we stroll through Mablethorpe as the night draws in. It is all razzamataz and bright flashing lights. Swinging ropes of bulbs link the street lights. Sounds of music are coming from amusements arcades and pubs along its main street; a mini Blackpool in fact. Diving into a narrow alley behind the main street is a surprise. There is nothing behind all the glitter and glamour. There are dustbins and debris, darkness and dreary broken walls and silence. The front street could have been a film set. This, says Mike is where he and his fellow 'Brylcream Boys' spent their off time when he was in the R.A.F. Words fail me. He assures me that it was a lot better when he was there! Forty years ago!

DAY 35. SUNDAY 28TH JULY
HULL VIA SALTFLEET AND GRIMSBY

I have to get my head around the fact that this is my last day. My trip is nearly over and soon my bags will be unpacked and 'normal service will be resumed as soon as possible.'

Following a hearty breakfast Mike says that this is where he is going to show me where he saved the nation or rather the east coast where he was stationed during his National Service. We drive about twelve miles or so along the coast. Every now and then over the years he has mentioned Theddlethorpe St Helen, which meant nothing to me but everything to him. Now he wants me to see exactly where he did sterling work for the R.A.F as a Radar Operator. We reach an isolated spot within sight of a village and its church and he then points to a field in which stands a large grey block of a building.

'Is this it?' I ask in surprise '

'This is it.' He replied with a sound of nostalgia in his voice.

'This is where you served the nation then?'

'Definitely' he said with feeling. 'And for several months too!' I could see that his memory was taking over.

We contemplate the building, once a barrack block. It didn't look so much a barrack block as a reinvented prison. I had been acquainted with several barrack blocks over the years and this didn't resemble any that I had slept in. 'What is it made of?' I queried.

'The walls were manufactured from wire netting sprayed with concrete.' he said, 'Perhaps it has been renovated since then.' He is always the optimist. Now its many windows look blank and dull against the grey of the walls.

'Did you actually enjoy your time here?' I was astonished that anyone could enjoy themselves in such a wasteland.

'Yes I did, There were about three dozen of us; most of us radar operators and radar mechanics, cooks and admin staff. We probably had a Warrant Officer and a Flight Sergeant as well.' He is still looking back to his R.A.F. days and I could see that whatever it looks like now he is still queuing for breakfast and chatting with his comrades doing bed parade.

'What did you do in the evenings or on your days off? There can't have been much to do around here. Did you have transport to get to Mablethorpe?' The area didn't look as if much traffic passed by.

'We had a lorry to take us in to Mablethorpe once a week and a bus service to Louth. That's where I went riding, it was great fun.' Obviously time away from this block would have been a highlight of the week.

'Anything else?' I asked, I simply can't get my head around the isolation.

‘Well when we got bored we counted the ducks crossing the road and some of the lads bet on the number going each way. When it got really exciting was when we took turns on guard duty at Donna Nook.’

‘Where on earth is that?’ There didn’t seem to be anything else in the vicinity.

‘Ah well you see Donna Nook is even more isolated than this, it does have a lot of wild life though’

‘That anywhere could be more desolate than this takes some beating.’ I remarked. I was nonplussed. Nowhere in sight was there a vestige of any other building. There was just a lot of nothing that I could see in any direction, the horizon was bare. It reminded me of Elphin when I stood for 50 minutes in the middle of nowhere.

We stood for some time looking at the forbidding building and Mike suggested that we went in and had a look round. It was obviously used for something as we could see a notice board on the front wall. As we approached it became clear: this was a care home for a number of people. The door opened and a gentleman came out to greet us and asked us if we would like to have a look round. We had no idea that it was now being used as a home and refuge for adults with minor mental problems. The structure hadn’t changed much in all those years. We were shown the public rooms, the dining room and office which wasn’t as bright and cheerful as I would have hoped. We left with the impression that if the residents’ bedrooms were of the same grey and beige colour that their time here wouldn’t have been very cheerful or more importantly very conducive to a state of mental well being..

I left feeling very depressed. That the building should have been used for a purpose was encouraging, but something more pleasant could have been thought up. A clinic for people to loose weight perhaps, Nobody could have popped down to the shops for a sneaky chocolate bar, there just weren’t any. Perhaps Mike felt the same although he had enjoyed his time out here – or so he said. Memory, like a sundial, can show only the sunny hours.

On the return journey to Mablethorpe for my penultimate bus we had a disagreement. He considered that I had successfully done what I had set out to do and it would be just as easy to return home and not complete the rest of my trip.

We had words, in fact several heated words.

I like to finish what I started, although I could see his point in that he would have to go into Hull and meet me following the bus if he didn't have to wait for me. I was adamant; I was going to finish the trip whether he came later or went straight to Hull. We examined the time table. I was prepared to give Saltfleetby St. Peter a miss as I was now running late and we would have to rush by car to catch the bus. There was a bus which I could catch without much waiting which would take me straight to Grismby and if I caught the bus that he had put in correctly we should meet up in Hull. In fact looking at the map there could even be a 'Race to the Finish'

He waited by the bus station and as I climbed aboard he got into the car and we were off. It was a pity that the bus route had to go inland for this leg of the journey as the countryside was not photogenic and in the main built up. Although I'm sure that there were some small interesting places along its route which we went through without stopping. North Coates and Tetney were just two of the villages that we passed on our way. There may have been more houses out of sight but I didn't think the bus driver could be persuaded to slow down sufficiently for me to enquire about photo opportunities and anyway there was a race on. Every now and then I tried to see if I could spot a red Skoda belting along either in front or trying to catch the bus and passing us. That day there was a dearth of red cars on the road and my neck was getting a crick in trying to spot my husband on the road.

I am bang on time as I reach Grimsby. Grimsby is not what I had expected; it was not at all a pleasing view of a town as one reaches it from the south. Although it is one of England's oldest towns having been granted a charter in 1201 by King John. The smell of the sea, especially fish straight from the sea, is all pervading even in a closed bus. A father further down the bus was pointing out to his son the 350 ft tower which was prominently situated at the dock gates. They really built things to impress in the eighteen hundreds. At the bus station which, with its aroma of fish, I had a job to locate the exact bus stand as some bright spark had been busy with a fibre pen. Nevertheless I am on my final bus and paid £2.95 for my last bus ticket and we are away to Hull. I can only hope that Mike has not been kept waiting or that he has got caught up in traffic on route. It is poetic that this last bus should run by 'Stagecoach' which has given me a feeling of been intrepid to the last!

The bus arrived dead on time and as I look out of the bus window I can see our red Skoda.

91 buses, 6 trains and 2 ferries to travel 3,000 miles.

The following pages are facsimiles of t
original timetables which I took with m

Sheet 1. W24 – F26 / MJJNY1-2 June
3 days/nights

Hull – ~~Eglinton~~ Edinburgh SYHA ~~nr Berwick on Tweed~~

date	depart	arrive	bbbtt	company	dist/time	
1 w 24/6 WED	hull; bus sta 1125+1225	scarbro'; somerset ter 1406+1506	M615 hrly	E Yks 121	58m 2.5hr 01482-327146	1
"	scarbro'; rwy sta 1430/40 +1602	whitby; bus sta 1532/42 + 1712	N119 2 hrly	tees 93/93a	20m 1hr 01642-444777	2
YHA B+B	whitby p142				meal @ 1900	78m
2 th 25/6 THUR	whitby; bus sta 953	middlesbro'; bus sta 1053	N119	tees 93/93a	32m 1hr as above	3
	middlesbro'; bus sta 1145	hartlepool; victoria rd 1229	N139 hrly	transit/Hpl 1/501	20m 3/4hr 01429-523555	4
	hartlepool; church sq 1252 + 1352	newcastle-on-t; bus sta 1443 + 1543	N401 hrly	Go-N / OK 31/231	30m 1 3/4hr 0845-606-0260	5
	newcastle;haymarket 1425 + (1625)	berwick-on-t; bus sta 1637 + ~~1837~~ 1842. Stand R	N495 (501)/505 &	nrthmbria 515/525	70m 2 1/4hr 01670-533128	6
	berwick; chapel st rwl st. 1730 + 1910	coldingham/St abbs 1800 + 2000	S101 hrly	CCconexions 235/251-253	12m 1/2hr	01289/308719 7
SYHA	coldingham (St Abbs)	p39	01890-771298		self cater	164m
3 F 26/6 FRI	St Abbs 0900 + 1000	eyemouth + berwick 0915 + 1015 / 0930 + 1030	S101	CCconexions 235/251-252		8
	eyemouth + berwick 0915+1015/1000+1300	edinburgh; bus sta 1200 + 1200	S105/107	CCconexions 251-256 Lowland 104	01289-308719 70m 2hr	9
SYHA	eglington p46	one of south edinburgh	0131-337-1120		meal	70m

File ~~has~~ Damaged – Do again

CICERONE'S

MARY BROWN
1 ORION TERRACE
... MILL
... HV6 ...

Keep

Sat 27—Tue 30 June Sheet 1 Edinburgh - Tongue

	date	depart	arrive	gbbtt	company	dist/time/tel
4	sat 27/6	**edinburgh; bus sta** 0920 + 0950 &c	**dundee; bus sta** 1200 + 1230 &c	S394/393 36m	fife scottish X60 + X59	36m 2 3/4hr 01592-642394
		dundee; bus sta 1310 + 1410	aberdeen; bus sta 1505 + 1603	S535	city link 965/969	70m 2hr 0990-505050
	SYHA	ABERDEEN SC	p21		01224-646988	total 106m
	Sun 28/6	**aberdeen; bus sta** 950	**elgin; bus sta** 1250	T135 aprox hrly	bluebird 305	69m 3hr 01224-212266
5		elgin; bus sta 1255 + 1355	inverness; bus sta 1410 + 1510	T243	invrnes traction 10	37m 2 1/4hr as above total 106m
	easy route	*aberdeen; bus sta* *1045*	*inverness; bus sta* *1410*	*T125*	*invrnes traction* *10*	*95m 3 1/2hr* *as above*
	SYHA	INVERNESS p69	meal			01463-231771
6	**mon 29/6**	**inverness; bus sta** 1330	**John o'Groats;harbo** 1715	T246	city link 958/959/960	80m 3 3/4hr
	SYHA	CANISBAY(Jn o' Gts)	SC p73			01955-611424
7	**tue 30/6**	**jn o'gts; hbr (canisby** 0740 + 1015	**thurso; rwy sta** 0847 + 1120	T255	harrold/Hi'ldCntr 280	20m 1hr 01955-631295
		Thurso;rwy/OlrigSt/PO **1055(PO)** + 1130	bettyhill - tongue 1204+1235, **1620(PO)**	T259/**F27**	various to btyhill postbT,F,S only	01463-256228
	SYHA	TONGUE SC p116	HOTEL as alternative		01847-611301	

\\
commu...
Bnk of
alng
Betty Hi...
PO 1.
TONG...

8.30 + 210 / 915 } stat...

9.52. 14/15: Uni...

Wed 1 – Sat 4 / Sun 5 July   Sheet ~~1~~ Tongue – L. Lomond (2 nts) 3

date	depart	arrive	gbbtt	company	dist/time/tel
wed 1/7	**tongue; PO** 935	lairg 1050	PO134	PO (14seat)	26m 1 1/4hr 01463-256288
	lairg 1215	elphin 1350	PO123	PO	as above
	elphin 1630	ullapool 1655	HI E55	spa/rapsons	10463-710555
SYHA	ULLAPOOL	p119 SC		01854-612254	
	see below for alternative route via Scourie on Wed to catch bus on Thurs fr Ullapool				
thur 2/7	**ullapool** 1530	acnasheen; rwy sta 1803	HI E54	invrnes traction 23	96m 2 1/2hr 01463-239292
	acnasheen; rwy sta 1915	kyle of lochalsh; rwy 2027	HI D15	SCOTRAIL	50m 1hr 0345-484950
	kyle of L; 2035 + 2101	kyleakin via skye br 2045 + 2110	HI D17	Hi'ld Cntry 355	2m 1/2hr 01478-612622
SYHA	KYLEAKIN p79 SC			01599-534585	
fri 3/7	**kyleakin** 0830/0835	armadale 0922 to catch FERRY	**HI D47**	Hi'ld Cntry 50/51	26m 3/4hr 01478-612622
	armadale FERRY 945	mallaig	HI D31	cal-mac ferry	8m 1/2hr 01678-462403
	mallaig 1210	fort william 1330	HI C71	citylink/sheil 919	44m 1 1/3hr 01847-893123
	ft william 1330Ss + 1800 **1705**	oban 1515Ss + 1935 **1935**	301 **217**	citylink 918 **919**	38m 1 3/4hr 0990-505050 **1 1/2hr**
SYHA	OBAN p96 snacks			01631-562025	
sat 4/7	**oban; rwy sta** 0800 + 1100 etc	arden;L.Lomond YH aprox1040 + 1410 &c	HI C18	citylink 975/976	75m 2 1/2hr 0990-505050
SYHA	LOCH LOMOND @ Arden	£8.60 + MEAL	for 2 nights	sat & sun 01389-850226	
	alternative route via Scourie		*to catch 1530 from ullapool*		
wed 1/7	**tongue 0935**	lairg 1050	PO134		
	lairg 1215	scourie 1420	PO 104		
B + B	SCOURIE				
thur 2/7	**scourie 0845**	elphin 0950	PO 129		
	elphin 1335	ullapool 1400	HI E55		

great place,

Is this Brigadoon?

Kids again

2 nights

There was NO FOOD in L Lomond!

Mon 6 - Wed 8 July Sheet L. Lomond - Chester

date	depart	arrive	gbbtt	company	dist/time/tel
mon 6/7	**L Lomond/Arden** approx 1015 CHECK	glasgow buchanan st 1100	HI/B11	city link 926/927	aprox 10m 3/4hr
	glasgow; buch'n'n st 1100 + 1200	stranraer, Pt rodie 1403 + 1515	R226 via ayr	western X 77	3hr 01563-525192
	stranraer; pt rodie 1705	dumfries: bus sta 1955	R117	various 500/501/ X75	3hr 0345-090510
B + B	DUMFRIES				
tue 7/7	**dumfries; bus sta** 920	carlisle; bus sta [illegible]	P161	western/cumbld 79/379	1 1/2hr as above
TRAIN	carlisle;RWY STA 1303	barrow;RWY STA 1529	cumbria B83	N W TRAINS	2 1/2hr 0345-484950
TRAIN	barrow;RWY STA 1645	lancaster;RWY ST 1744	cumbria	N W TRAINS	**1hr**
B + B	LANCASTER				
Wed 8/7	**Lancaster;bus sta** 0854 + 0953	**blackpool; bus sta** 1003 + 1103	K663	stagecoach lancs X42/42	1hr 01257-241693
	blackpool; bus sta 1020 + 1120	preston; bus sta 1200 + 1300	K633	ribble 167/168	1 3/4hr 01257-241-693
	preston; bus sta 1230 + 1330	[illegible]	K649	ribble [illegible]/102/702	1 3/4hr 01257-24158[illegible]
	southport; lord st 1437 + 1537	chester: bus sta 1635 + 1735	K417	crossville/NW X8	2hr 01244-602666
YHA	CHESTER p112	meal 1800-1930	page112	01244-680056	

13 14 15

TIC. 01387 25838

TIC. 01524 328

TIC. 01244 4021

FULL

Lancaster

01387 Dumfries

Armstrong
7 TERREGLES St.
257018.

mrs Rankin
& Cassalans
261806.

mrs Steadmeyer
North LAUREK Place.
252368

Thur 9 - Mon 13 July Sheet ~~1~~ Chester - Bath (2 nts @ Tenby) 5

date	depart	arrive	gbbtt	company	dist/time/tel	
thur 9/7	**chester; bus exch** 0820 + hrly	rhyll bus+rwy sta 1010 + hrly	K433 walesM23	crosville cymru A1/A8	30m 2hr 01745-343721	Bus (A1 RHY
	rhyll bus+rwy sta 1035 + aprox 1/2hrly	llandudno: palladium 1141	J131 wales L51	C/V = crosville 14/15/16	15m 1 1/3hr 01492-596969	
YHA	llandudno;penllyn,bst 1645 ask if others <u>BANGOR p 102</u>	bangor; clock (YHA) 1746 meal @ 1900	J271 wales J97	CV 5/5A/5B 01248-353516	14m 1hr as above	
fri 10/7	**bangor; clock** 9.50 ~~1005~~	porthmadog 1110	H471	CV + rhondda 701(cardiff bus)	1hr	£4.50
TRAIN	porthmadog; Ff rwy 1245	minffordd/portmeirion 1255 visit portmeirion	wales J15	Ffestioniog rwy	10min 01765-514715	
TRAIN YHA	minffordd; rwy sta 1527 + 1713 <u>LLANBEDR p106</u>	llanbedr: rwy sta 1542 + 1732 meal @ 1900	wales J11	central trains 01341-241287	20min 0345-484950	mustn't forget to stop train
sat 10/7 TRAIN	**llanbedr; rwy sta** 0818 ~~844~~	machynlleth; rwy st 1001	wales J11	central trains	1 3/4hr as above	MURIEL
TRAIN	machynlleth; rwy sta 1042	aberystwyth; rwy sta 1114	wales H11	central trains	18m 1/2hr	
	aberyswyth: rwy sta 1305	cardigan: finch's sq 1448	H473 wales 53	CV/richards 550	1 3/4hr 01267-231817	
	cardigan; finch's sq 1505	haverfordwest;bussta 1633/1636	H463	richards bros 412	1 1/2hr as above	
B + B	haverfordwest;bussta 1745 <u>TENBY via TIC</u>	tenby; south parade 1911 *stay 2 nights sat + sun*	H433	SWT/silcox	where we were	gone? 2 nights
mon 13/7 YHA	**tenby; uppr park rd** 1145 <u>BATH p42</u>	bristol - bath 1510 1545 meal 1700 - 1930 01225-465674	H299	SWT 100/302	4hrs 01792-580580	£6.58

firm scottle 16 tel ow 17 18/19 20

£4.40

In Tenby try Plantaganet Restaurant nr Harbour

TIC Tenby

remember to charge phone.

Bath – Perranporth
Sheet 6

Sheet 6 : Tues 14 – Th 16 July
Bath 3 days/nights

date	depart	arrive		gbbtt	company	dist/time/tel
TUE 21 T 14/7	**bath spa rwysta**	0848	0939 (Bath arrive 10.20)	1001 (Bristol)	1158	TRAINS
	bristol temple md rwy	0907	0955 (ARR)			"
	as above	0946	1010 (Bristol dep)			
	weston s mere rwy	1007	query	1040		
	as above					
	bridgwater rwy sta		1042 (arrive)		1237	
	above journey by bus	depends on 3 to 5 minute gaps between connexions at diff stations				
choice of weston s mere; centre	1100	bridgwater; E Quay 1225		B531	badger 102	20m 1 1/2hr 0117-955-3231
or	bridgwater; bus sta 1340 (bus)	minehead; parade 1515		B524	south'n national 15	27m 1 1/2hr 01823-272033
	minehead; bancks st 1620	ilfracombe; bus sta 1825		B242	S Nat./red bus 300	38m 2hr 01271-45444
YHA	ILFRACOMBE p49	meal @ 1900		(YHA MINEHEAD p53)		total 110m
WED 22 W 15/7	**Ilfracombe; high st** 0823 + 1023	**barnstaple, bus sta** 0854 + 1054		B224	red bus 30	14m 1/2hr 01271-45444
	barnstaple; bus sta 0855 + 1255	bideford; quay 0920 + 1320		B239	red bus 319	10m 1/2hr 01392-382800
	bideford; quay 1115 + 1550	bude; the strand 1240 + 1715		B237	red bus 85	27m 1 1/2hr as above
	bude; the strand 1330, 1710 + 1900	boscastle; bridge 1400. 1740 + 1930		B174	western national 122/125	17m 1/2h 01209-719988
YHA	BOSCASTLE	p43 meal @ 1900				total 70m
THUR 23 TH 16/7	**boscastle; bridge** 0735 + 0920	**wadebridge;bus sta** 0840 + 1025		B174	as above 122/125	17m 1hr as above
	wadebridge; bus sta 0936 + 1056	padstow; bus sta 1005 + 1125		B172	as above 55 + 122	10m 1/2hr as above
	padstow; bus sta 1000 + 1305	newquay 1120 + 1425			west'n nat 56	16m 1 1/3hr as above
	newquay; east st 1320 + 1620	perranporth;beach rd 1420 + 1655		B160	as above 57/57D	6m 1/2hr 01209-719988
YHA	PERRANPORTH p55					total 50 m

the 1620 bus goes onto St Ives (stay @ B+B) ETA 1830 & to Penzance YHA 1905 p54

Margin notes: 21 · 22 out confirm · 23 what bus? · John · phone · confirm Thur · 23.7 · 24.3

p49 Ilfracombe 01271-865337

p43 Boscastle 01840-250287

File – LOST My Ser Sea

p55 Perranporth 01872-573812

p54 Penzance 01326-311435
has cafeteria see p54

p53 Minehead 01643-702595

Keep

Fri 17 – Sun 19 July   ~~Sheet1~~ Perranporth (or) Penzance } → { Beer (or) Lyme Regis ?

date	depart	arrive	gbbtt	company	dist/time/tel
fri 17/7	perranporth;beach rd 1055	St Ives; malakoff 1220	B160	west'n nat 57/57D	26m 1 1/2hr 01209-719988
	Sy Ives; malakoff 1350	land's end 1520	B105	west'n national 15	25m 1 1/2hr as above
Change St Ives	land's end <u>1615</u> + 1725	penzance; bus sta ~~1705~~ 1720 + 1820	B101	west'n nat 1/1A/1B/1C	10m 1hr as above
<u>YHA</u>	<u>PENZANCE p54</u>	cafeteria from 1730		~~01326-311435~~ 01736 362666	Total 71m
sat 18/7	penzance;bus sta 1005	helston; coinage hall st 1051	B108	west'n nat 2	13m 50min as above
	helston; woolwoths 1140	truro; the green 1227	B115	truronian T1	17m 50min 01872-273453
	truro; bus sta 1425	St Austell;rwy sta/Par St A 1510 / Par 1539	B142	west'n nat 24A	14m 3/4hr 01209-719988
TRAIN	St Austell;rwy sta m-f 1535+1625 <u>S1604</u> *trains also run from Par, the next sta*	plymouth;rwy sta m-f 1629+1732 S1638			0345-484950
<u>YHA</u>	<u>PLYMOUTH p55</u>	meal 1900		01752-562189	
sun 19/7	plymouth; bus sta 0935 + 1205	dartmouth; pontoon 1145 + 1415	B351	west'n nat 93	36m 2 1/4hr 01752-222666
FERRY to kingswear	as bus stops @ ferry pontoon its logical that ferry waits for bus. CHECK				bus waits 4 ferry
	kingswear; banjo 1145 + 1415	torquay; strand 1228 + 1458	B450	stagecoachDevon 200	10m 3/4hr 01803-613226
	torquay; strand 1330 + 1530	exeter; bus sta 1425 + 1625	B441	stagecoachDevon X46	26m 1hr as above
	exeter; bus sta 1511 + 1611	sidmouth; triangle 1545 + 1646	B414	stagecoachDevon 52/52A/52B	12m 35min as above
	sidmouth; triangle 1705 last bus on Sun	BEER b4 seaton 1737 lyme regis;square 1825	B475	south western 378	7-15m 1/2-1 1/3 01392-382800
<u>YHA</u>	<u>BEER p42 b4 seaton</u>	meal 1900		01297-20296	
<u>B + B</u>	LYME REGIS x				
	day off 2 nights in one or both places BUT must be in Lyme for early bus depart to make connections thru' to Portsmouth in one day				P.T.O.

£6.53

TIC 01297 442138

28.17

2 nights

If staying @ Beer YH – suggest walk over cliffs to Lyme Regis – approx 7 miles (ask @ Hostel) – on Monday

MRS Endersby.
Rolterfield
View Rd. Lyme Regis

£16 50 p.n.
01297 445585.

Sheet 8 Tues 21 July

Mon (Day 28) 20/7

Sheet 8 Seaton (Beer) Lyme Regis — Portsmouth (Cosham)

date	depart	arrive	gbbtt	company	dist/time/tel
Tues21/7	**seaton;triangle**(beer) 0900 + 1000 if fr YHA	lyme regis;PO 1048 + 1048	B473	axe valley 899	7m 3/4hr 01392-382800
NOTE	*recommended to stay night in B+B lyme regis to catch early bus to reach Portsmouth*				
Tues 21/7	**lyme regis; PO** **0938** + 1138	weymouth;king's statue 1115 + 1315	B511	Southern Nat'l 41/31X	29m 1 1/2hr 01823-272033
	weymouth;king's statue **1240** + 1525	poole; bus sta 1420 + 1[illegible]0	B754	wilts & dorset 187/188/189	30m 1 3/4hr 01202-673555
	poole; bus sta *every 5 to 10 mins*	bournemouth;square *1/2hr jny*	B761	wilts+dst=W+D 101/102/103/105	1/2hr
	bournemouth;**triangle** **1525** + 1725	southampton;castle way 1709 + 1957	C101	W+D/BlueLine X1 + X2	as above
	S'hmpton;PoundTreeRd **1740**	portsmouth;the hard 1815	C557	S'hmptonCityBus 727/747	

NOTE as Portsmouth ***(Cosham)*** *YHA is on N edge of town entailing local bus out recommended you take TRAIN from Southampton(or Bournemouth)to* ***Cosham rwy sta*** *10min walk from YHA*

to cosham

TRAIN	southampton; rwy sta **1744** + 2044	cosham;rwy sta 1823 + 2123	✓
YHA	PORTSMOUTH (cosham) c34 [illegible] al 1900	01705-375661	

3 9 5 c 0

not at stn — ✓

2 ℓ

Booked ✓

missed meal.

look for ghosts @ Wymering

those wardens!

why did I do this? — ask for helicopter!

Filed A Tj S Eng

Sheet 9 Wed 22 July + Thur 23 July

COSHAM (P/Mth) – Dover
Dover – Blaxhall

date	depart	arrive	gbbtt	company	dist/time/tel
today's journey from portsmouth to dover has a 3 1/2hr bus jny to brighton plus a 5hr bus to dover suggest either stay (a) o'night @ brighton (YHA @ patcham p28) or transfer @ brighton to dover bus & stop off @ eastbourne YHA p30 or hastings YHA p31 & catch same bus to dover in morning This may mess up other days! **Vital to book S coast YHAs well in advance**					
Altrernative go by train part way from Portsmouth to Brighton, Eastbourne or Hastings					
wed 22/7	**portsmouth;the hard** 0845, **0915** + 0945 *alternative get local bus or train cosham to havant bus sta for same bus 1/2hr later*	brighton; pool valley 1210, 1240 + 1310	D709 1/2hrly	coastline 700	45m 3 1/2hr 0345-959099
	havant; bus sta 0917, **0947** + 1017	brighton(b'ton)as above		as above	
	brighton; churchill sq **1240 + 1340** *bus via newhaven, eastbourne, hastings, rye & lydd* if you start early fr portsmouth you can take time to get off for an hr & catch next bus	dover; pencester rd 1730 + 1830	D779 hrly	South Coast 711	90m 5 hr 0345-581457
TRAIN 2 changes	**cosham; rwy sta** 0953 hrly *and take above bus fr eastbourne(Arndale Centre) or hastings (Breeds Place) to dover*	arrive havant dep 0957 hrly 1010 hrly 1300hrly → 1630 @	arr b'ton (Brighton) dep 1112 hrly 1124	**eastbourne** 1157 hrly	**hastings** 1227hrly 1305 hrly → 1530 Dover
YHA	DOVER p29 meal 1830-1930	Dover 01304-201314			
thur 23/7 £9.00	**dover; pencester rd** 0845 + 0915 **dover; bus sta** 940	london; victoria bus sta D028 1120 + 1150 london; victoria bus sta 1220		Nat Express 0 two 0	0990-808080
	essential book in advance by telephone or thru' agent or bus sta				
£800	london; victoria bus sta 1430 only bus of day	ipswich, bus sta 1700		Nat Express 0 eight one	as above
1700	ipswich; bus sta 1745	Stratford St Andrew approx 1837	E310	E Cnties 80/99 E Nat'l 124/166	15m 55min 0645-583358
YHA	walk 1 mile down lane (for Tunstall) to BLAXHALL p62 meal 1900	01728-688206			

30.250

Train all the way get train Brighton train from Brighton to Hastings

Bus from Hastings 5 mins every

BREEDS place

filed A TTj London

Sheet 10 — Fri/Sat 24/25 July — Blaxhall – Sheringham
SUN 26/7 — Sheet — Sheringham – Hunstanton
Mon 27/7 — Hunstanton – Mablethorpe

date	depart	arrive	gbbtt	company	dist/time/tel
Fri 24/7	*walk fr Blaxhall 1mile to Tunstall for TT E309 or to Stratf'd St And for E 310/312*				
	Tunstall PO 946	Saxmundhamgarage 1010	E309	various	6m 25min 0345-583358
OR	**Stratford**St Andrews 0930 + 1030 approx	Saxmundhamgarage 0945 + 1050	E310	E Cnties 80/99 E Nat'l 124/166	6m 15min as above
	saxmundham;High st 1044 + 1244	lowestoft bus sta 1227 + 1427	E312	E Cnties 99	25m 1 3/4hr as above
31/32	lowestoft; bus sta **1305** + 1705	Grt Yarmouth;Mkt Pl 1336 + 1800	E618	Cambridge 74	10m 25min 0600-626116
OR	**1345** + 1445	1419 + 1519	E463 hrly	Blue Bus 600	as above
YHAs in Grt Yarmouth p64 M1900; Norwich p67 M1800-1915 & Sheringham p68 M1800-1930	01493-843991	01603-627647		01263-823215	
	GrtYarm'th;Mkt gates **1538** (0950 fast 1408)	Norwich bus sta **1638** (1038 fast 1503)	E403 M-F only	Blue bus 701/702/705	20m 50-60min 0500-626116
	norwich; bus sta 1525, 1605 & 1815	sheringham; rwy sta 1659, 1723 & 1927	E421 M-S only	E Cnties 58/58X	30m approx 1hr as above
YHA	SHERINGHAM p68	meal 1900, 1930 std. 2 nights here or 1 here & another in Norwich			2 nights
				coastline bus	
Sun 26/7	**sheringham**sta appr 0850 + 1150	hunstanton; bus sta 1034 + 1400	E500	various	38m 0500-626116
YHA	HUNSTANTON p65	meal 1900 01485-532061		01553-772461 (or go on to King's Lynn YHA self catering)	
SUN cont	hunstanton; bus sta 20' past 11,12,14+15	king's lynn;bus/rwy 8' past 12,13,15+16hrs	E475 hrly	E Cnties 410/411	12m 50min as above
Mon 27/7	**hunstanton**; bus sta 0925, 0930 & 1000	king's lynn; bus/rwy 1015, 1015 & 1045	E475	as above	as above
OR	**king's lynn**; bus sta 1035 + 1135	spalding; bus sta 1200 + 1300	L579 hrly	fowler travel & cavalier no. 00	24m 1 1/2hr 01522-553135
easy route	*spalding; bus sta 1515 (via skegness @ 1630)*	*mablethorpe;seacroft 1700*		Nat Express 419 book ahead	0900-808080
B + B	MABLETHORPE				

local buses fr Spalding hourly @ 45 & 55 mins past hour arriving Boston @ 38 mins past next hr to connect from Boston Bus Sta @1106,1410 + 1615 to Skegness [redacted]/*LincolnRd1218,1546,1722* leaving Skegness Bus Sta @ 1410 + 1610 arriving Mablethorpe @ 1515 + 1715
Scenes of my RAF youth, see M/thorpe & die! ALL Tel. 01522-553135

a) L571/L575 various
b) L559 Brylaine B10/RoadCar
c) L483 RoadCar 90

filed A-Z; E Ang on A

Tues 28 July

Sheet 1 Mablethorpe - Sby Br. via Hull   11

date	depart	arrive	gbbtt	company	dist/time/tel
Tues 28/7	**mablethorpe**; Vic Rd 0930 + 1030	**saltfleetby**; St Clements ?? approx 0940 + 1040 ?	L485	grayscroft no 1	10m 10min 01507-473236
NOTE *this service (to Louth) may go beyond Saltfleetby calling at Saltfleet & N Somercotes before runningback to turn off at Saltfleetby St Clements for Louth.* **Ascertain from driver where you get off to catch the bus** (starting Saltfleetby St Peter) ***for Grimsby*** and passing through Saltfleetby St Clements, Saltfleet & N Somercotes. *You may need to go as far North as possible to make connexion* **You may have to walk 2 miles fr Sfltby St C to Saltfleet !**					
	saltfleetby st peter 1150	grimsby; bus sta 1250	L633	applebys 00	20m 1hr 01472-348421
	grimsby; bus sta 1300, 1330, 1400 etc	HULL bus sta 1400, 1430,1500	L628 1/2 hrly	stagecoach express 909	33m 1hr 01472-385646
B + B	SOWERBY BRIDGE	**welcome home do you want fetching fr hull or ?**			

6

Mike - please check later
or I will Sat.
Does the X312 X449 from Mablethorpe
go straight thro to Grimsby.
(only on a Tues)
Nice driver - 10 am = Grimsby 11.15
£3-75.

Grimsby - Hull Stagecoach E.
~~12.3~~ 12.30. 1.30.
~~£4 50~~. £2-95.

350 32.
65
50
351.47

and it could be done -

Acknowledgements

First and foremost I would like to thank my dear and patient husband Michael who persuaded me to do it in the first place. He spent weeks overcoming early frustration to achieve immense satisfaction in compiling the timetables. Without his diligence my adventure could not have taken place. he was always on the other end of a phone giving support especially when I hit my lowest ebb.

To Lydia who spent a whole hour putting all my photos in to a memory stick.

To Esma O'Neill of Simprint in Sowerby Bridge who put the whole thing together, understood what I wanted, had bright ideas of her own and was so enthusiastic about the project. Front cover design by Danielle Rowley at Simprint.

This book would never have been written had it not been for Sheila Mellings, of the Pennine Wine Circle, whose persistence in requesting 'The Book' bullied me to turning both my tour notes and my talk into print.

Lightning Source UK Ltd.
Milton Keynes UK
UKHW010751201219
355695UK00001B/58/P

9 781839 450761